PERCY CANE

Garden Designer

Percy Cane

PERCY CANE

Garden Designer

RONALD WEBBER

John Bartholomew & Son Ltd   Edinburgh

BY THE SAME AUTHOR

The Early Horticulturists
Covent Garden: Mud Salad Market
The Village Blacksmith
Market Gardening: The History of Commercial Flower,
Fruit, and Vegetable Growing

First published in Great Britain 1975
by John Bartholomew & Son Ltd.
12 Duncan Street, Edinburgh EH9 1TA
and at: 216 High Street, Bromley BR1 1PW

ISBN 0 70281 080 0

Printed in Great Britain by
Biddles Ltd., Guildford, Surrey

Contents

Preface

'The bare ground is our canvas, and shrubs and trees, flowers and stones are the paints. It rests with the artist to create scenes of perfect beauty, or to obtain results of less charm. Every group of trees may in itself be a picture, and the beds and borders can give successions of beautiful forms, and of lovely combinations of colours . . . The completed whole may be one changing scene of loveliness, every part of it varying in colour and light with every hour of the day, and with every day of the year.'

Thus wrote a young garden architect during the dark days of the First World War. Over fifty years later—by which time he had become the distinguished doyen of British garden designers—the same man could write (in an introduction to one of his books, *The Creative Art of Garden Design*): 'Designing gardens is an art, but as in painting, the man who knows little about art but knows what he likes, enjoys a picture that observes certain basic principles. As in all the arts there are periods of growth and of changing fashion, but the principles remain constant. To make a beautiful garden the gardenmaker must know not only what he is doing, but also why he is doing it.'

Must know not only what he is doing, but also why he is doing it. Of no man could this be said more justly than of the author of these lines, Percy Cane, who is the subject of this book. Percy Cane remained faithful to these basic principles throughout his long career (he retired in 1973 at the age of 91) and his gardens, to be found in several continents, are there to prove it. Palace gardens at Falkland in Scotland and at Addis Ababa in Ethiopia, gardens at Dartington Hall in England and at a world fair in America, and many hundreds of others all bearing his imprint will suffice to ensure that Percy Cane takes his rightful place among the famous British garden architects of the past.

I have been privileged to write this book: but I could never have done so without the active co-operation (in the early stages of the manuscript) of

Mr. Cane himself—particularly in the loan of his memoirs which he had already prepared. I would also like to thank Miss Enid Caldicott, Mr. J. F. Crittall, Mr. E. F. Dowling, Dr. John Elliott, Mr. Arthur Hellyer, Mr. A. G. Healey, Mr. Robert Pearson, and many others who have helped with information or advice, and also the owners of the gardens illustrated in the book for the use of photographs and plans of their gardens. Many of the plans were drawn by Mr. Harold White who did a lot of work for Mr. Cane over the years. My thanks, too, to the Royal Horticultural Society Library, the British Museum Reading Room, the Essex County Library at Chelmsford, and Camden Library, for their assistance.

RONALD WEBBER

1
Early Days

Stephen Percy Cane, international garden designer, author, editor and journalist, was born on 20 September 1881 at Bocking Mill, a pleasant roomy house standing in its own grounds bordering the river at Bocking, near Braintree in Essex.

Bocking at that time, though still a village, was rapidly changing under the influence of the flourishing artificial silk business which had been brought there at the end of the eighteenth century by Samuel Courtauld. Percy (as he was always called) was the eldest of five children: he had a brother, John Wagstaff, and three sisters, Irene, Amy Ellen, and Evelyn.

The young Percy learned to love the river, for the family possessed both a boat and a canoe. He regularly went for a row before breakfast. Sailing, however (the boat was large enough to take five and have a sail), could be tricky, for the river was narrow and rapid tacking was called for to avoid collision with the river banks. Close to the orchard the river turned sharply—almost at a right angle—and, as water does when flowing round a bend, had washed out a hole in the river bank. One day Percy, out in the boat with a friend, decided to bathe at this hole. It could have been the end of him and this story would never have been written. His legs became entangled with strong water-lilies which coiled round him in the way in which, Percy felt, an octopus would have gone to work. What was worse, he could not make his companion, who was safe and comfortable in the boat, realise the danger. No one but himself ever knew how he felt, trapped like this. But after quite a struggle he managed to extricate himself, and with a feeling of overwhelming relief swam to the bank and safety.

Percy's father was good at most outdoor activities and encouraged his children to lead active and healthy lives. Two ponies provided much enjoyment as well as exercise: often the ponies were ridden tandem, Percy and sister Amy on one, brother Jack and Irene on the other. There was also a tennis court. Percy particularly liked walking, riding and rowing. But he was never keen on organised sports. He felt they were a waste of valuable time but this might have been because he was not very good at them. Even more he disliked watching sport, feeling that one should not spend time as a mere passive spectator.

One of the outbuildings at Bocking Mill was a barn, used as a potting shed, with a loft over it to which access was gained by a rickety staircase. Here Percy was allowed to do as he wished. He covered the windows, for instance, with fine wire mesh netting and kept canaries; on the floor he had some Belgian Hare rabbits. The potting shed proper was more the domain in those days of Percy's mother who was a keen gardener. She was particularly good at the Victorian style of bedding out. Her begonias, according to her son, were really fine and her geraniums startling in their vivid colours.

A love of gardening manifested itself fairly early in the life of the young Cane. He liked handling soil and had his own small plot in the family kitchen-garden, divided into four separate parts by gravel paths neatly edged with dwarf box. He sowed seeds, planted out seedlings and grew plants such as geraniums, dahlias, asters and various other annuals—laying, in fact, the foundation of what was to be a lifetime spent among gardens. He also liked moving plants and shrubs though he admits that this was not always to their benefit. He bought seeds from a local nurseryman who could not have been overjoyed to see him for if he had a shilling to spend he would generally make two journeys over the spending.

At an early age Percy was sent to a nursery school under the care of a Miss Shearcroft whom he remembers as 'a lady of severe aspect, who from the first always frightened me.' Next he went to an establishment run by Lygon Graham Pakenham, a member of the Irish Longford family, and considered the best private school for boys in the district. Here Percy enjoyed the study side more than the games. He was a bright pupil, one of the brightest at the school: in fact he was top boy on several occasions. In addition he unconsciously became imbued with the high ethical standards that were enforced at the school and in years to come he was to be grateful for these standards which became part of his mental and moral make-up.

He experienced most of the ups and downs of normal childhood. When he was about twelve, for instance, his father bought another house on the outskirts of Braintree. Here the river ran close to the house with a consequent danger of flooding. Percy was sent, while the house was being decorated, to sleep in it alone. 'I'm sure my father had no idea of the torture it was to me to be alone in that rambling room,' he said in later years. 'I slept on a camp bed and moved from room to room as the workmen got on with the decorating and repairing. I was almost too terrified at times to turn over in bed.' But he told no one of this at the time for he was afraid of being thought a coward.

Occasionally he went to stay with relations 'for what were supposed to have been pleasure visits.' He liked going to his paternal grandfather's place because his youngest aunt who lived there had a studio which generated an artistic atmosphere which even at that early age Percy found most congenial. He loved the smell of paint which permeated the studio and liked listening to his aunt playing the piano. The sound of a piano was always music to his ears as long as it was not 'pop' or jazz music. But his aunt was an accomplished performer and he never heard her play a note of second-rate music.

A visit to an uncle, however, was not so pleasant. This uncle owned a large printing works and it was understood (though never stated in so many words) that Percy would go and live with this uncle and aunt, who had no children, and in return for comforting their declining years would inherit the printing works. He accepted an invitation to visit them even at that stage of the proceedings with many forebodings. The first evening passed slowly and Percy went to bed early. The next morning he was shown over the printing works which he found quite interesting and went back to lunch in a fairly cheerful frame of mind. Then came another evening and for one who was used to animated conversation at home 'it was terrible.' His mind was soon made up. Not for all the printing works in the world could he live that kind of life! But how to get out of the situation without offending his uncle and aunt who were kindness itself? Finally he crept from the house and, going to the nearest post-office, sent a telegram home telling his parents how he felt and asking for a way out of the situation. The following morning he was tremendously relieved to see his mother arrive with many presents and kind messages for the uncle and aunt but with the announcement that she was taking Percy back with her, and that she and her husband did not think that their son was cut out for a life in printing.

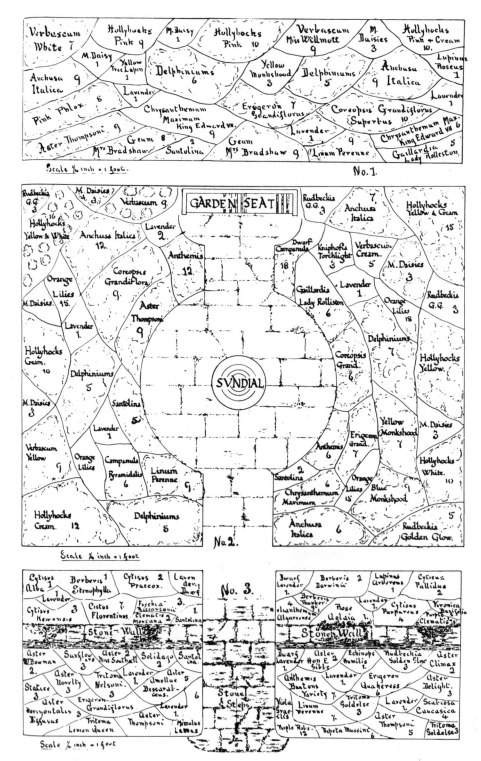

No. 1

Verbascum White 7 · Hollyhocks Pink 9 · M.Daisy 1 · Hollyhocks Pink 10 · Verbascum Miss Willmott 9 · M. Daisies 3 · Hollyhocks Pink & Cream 10. · Lupinus Roseus 1 · M.Daisy 1 · Yellow Tree Lupin 1 · Delphiniums 6 · Yellow Monkshood 3 · Delphiniums 5 · Anchusa Italica 9 · Lavender 1 · Anchusa Italica 9 · Lavender 1 · Pink Phlox 8 · Chrysanthemum Maximum King Edward VII 9 · Erigeron Grandiflorus 7 · Coreopsis Grandiflorus Superbus 10 · Chrysanthemum Max. King Edward VII 6 · Aster Thompsoni 9 · Geum 8 Mrs Bradshaw 2 Santolina · Geum Mrs Bradshaw 9 · Lavender 1 · Linum Perenne 9 · Gaillardia Lady Rolleston 5

Scale ¾ inch = 1 foot.

No. 2

GARDEN SEAT

SUNDIAL

Rudbeckia G.G. 3 · M. Daisies 3 · Verbascum 9 · Rudbeckia G.G. 3 · Anchusa Italica 7 · Hollyhocks Yellow & Cream · Hollyhocks Yellow & White 16 · Anchusa Italica 12 · Lavender 2 · Dwarf Campanula 18 · Kniphofia Torchlight 3 · Verbascum Cream 5 · M. Daisies 3 · 15 · Orange Lilies 15 · Coreopsis Grandiflora 9 · Anthemis 12 · Gaillardia Lady Rolliston 6 · Lavender 1 · Orange Lilies 18 · Rudbeckia G.G. 3 · M.Daisies 15 · Aster Thompsoni 9 · Lavender 1 · Hollyhocks Cream 10 · Delphiniums 5 · Santolina 5 · Coreopsis Grand. 6 · Delphiniums 7 · Hollyhocks Yellow · M.Daisies 3 · Lavender 1 · Yellow Monkshood 7 · M.Daisies 3 · Verbascum Yellow 9 · Orange Lilies · Campanula Pyramidalis 6 · Linum Perenne 9 · Anthemis 6 · Erigeron Grand. 7 · Hollyhocks White 10 · Santolina 6 · Orange Lilies 15 · Blue Monkshood · 5 · Hollyhocks Cream 12 · Delphiniums 8 · Chrysanthemum Maximum 2 · Anchusa Italica 6 · Rudbeckia Golden Glow.

Scale ½ inch = 1 foot

No. 3

Cytisus Alba 1 · Berberis Stenophylla · Cytisus 2 Praecox. · Lavendev dev. Dwarf · Cytisus Kewensis · Cistus 7. Florentinus · Fuchsia 3 Riccartonii · Clematis 2 Montana · Santolina · Stone Wall · Aster W.Bowman 2. · Sunflower 3 · Aster 2 Miss Southall · Solidago 1 Santolina · Statice 3 · Aster Novelty 3 · Tritonia Nelsoni · Lavender 1 · Anthemus 3 Bessaralceus · Aster Bessaral- ceus 6 · Aster Horizontalis Jiggasus 3 · Erigeron Grandiflorus · Lavender · Aster Thompsoni · Mimulus Lamus · Tritoma Lemon Queen

Dwarf Lavender 1. · Berberis 2 Darwinii · Lupinus Arboreus 1 · Cytisus Pallidus 2 · Helianthemum Algarvense · Berberis 4 Thunberg 1. · Rose Aglaia 1. · Lavender 1. · Cytisus Purpureus 4 · Veronica 3 Prostrata · Purple 4 Clematis · Stone Wall · Dwarf Lavender 1 · Aster Hon E. Gibbs 2 · Echinops Humilis · Rudbeckia Golden Glow · Aster Climax 2 · Anthemis Buxtons Variety 7. · Lavender 1 · Erigeron Quakeress · Aster Delight. · Viola Gracellis · Linum Perenne 7. · Tritoma Goldelse 1. · Lavender 1. · Scabiosa Caucasica 4 · Purple Rose 12 · Nepeta Mussini 3 · Aster Thompsoni 5 · Tritoma Goldelse 3

Stone Steps

Scale ½ inch = 1 foot

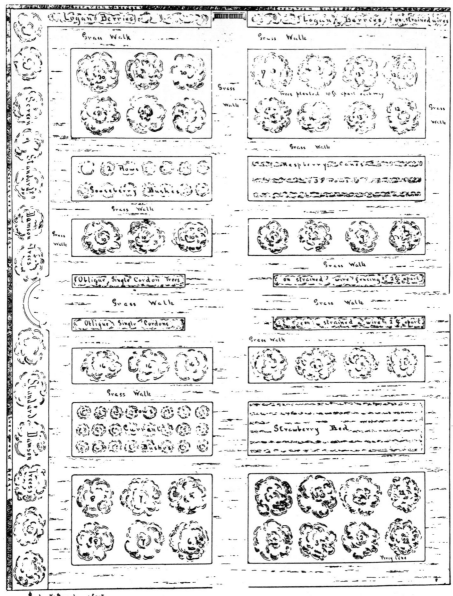

Suggestions for an orchard. Another 1915 design

Opposite: One of Percy Cane's earliest published garden designs.
In My Garden, Illustrated, *October, 1915*

A pen and ink drawing from My Garden, Illustrated *in 1916*

A paved garden. Drawn in 1916

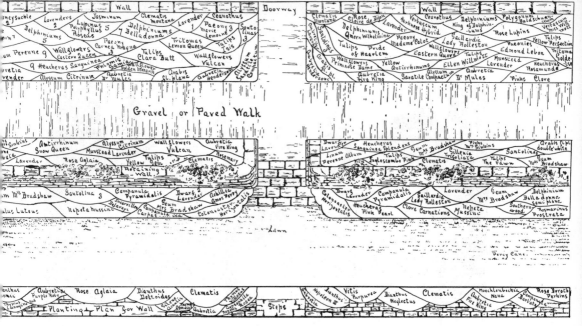

Flower border varieties during World War I

An idea for a bungalow garden, 1916

Vol. VIII., No. 46.   MAY, 1918.   Monthly, 6d. Net.

EDITED BY PERCY S. CANE, F.R.H.S.

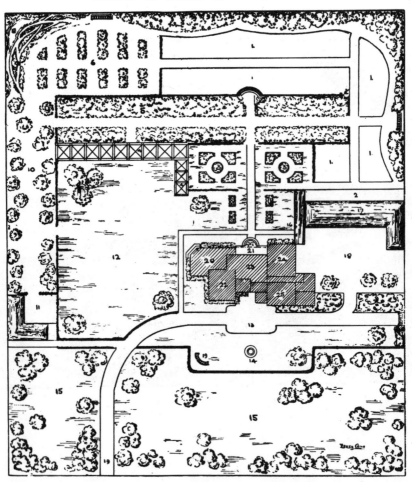

A COUNTRY COTTAGE AND GARDEN.

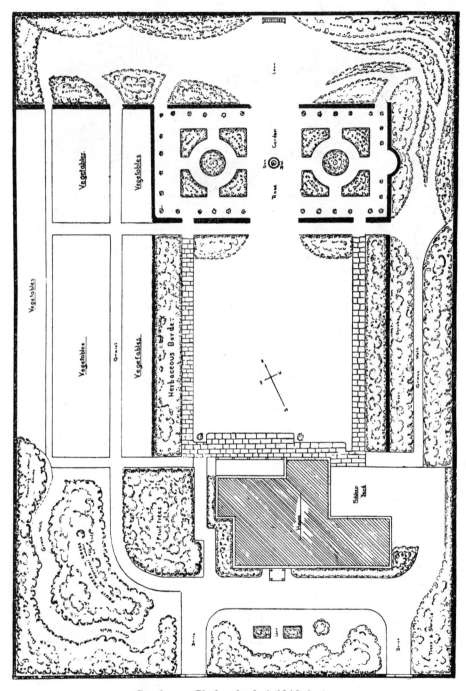

Garden at Chelmsford. A 1918 design

Opposite: The cover of the first issue of My Garden, Illustrated
to be edited by Percy Cane

Paved court and fruit wall, 1918

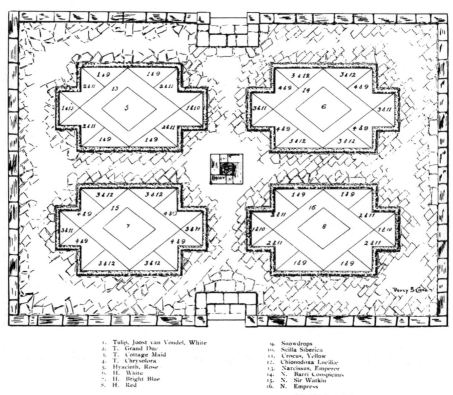

1. Tulip, Joost van Vondel, White
2. T. Grand Duc
3. T. Cottage Maid
4. T. Chrysolora
5. Hyacinth, Rose
6. H. White
7. H. Bright Blue
8. H. Red

9. Snowdrops
10. Scilla Siberica
11. Crocus, Yellow
12. Chionodoxa Luciliæ
13. Narcissus, Emperor
14. N. Barri Conspicuus
15. N. Sir Watkin
16. N. Empress

Copyright - Percy S. Cane

Spring planting plan for a small Dutch garden, 1919

Design for a stairway, 1920

Though Percy was in later years to go to many places which he was glad to leave never did he pack his case with so much speed and so joyfully as he did on that occasion. Every line in his face, he felt, took on an upward curve, but if his uncle and aunt noticed it they were too polite to say anything.

He often spent summer holidays with two other aunts, one married but childless, the other a dear old lady of about sixty years of age. They were very kind to him and took him out to tea when they went to call on other ladies similarly situated. He liked this fairly well but when he could he escaped to the kitchen to have tea there. In the kitchen he did not have to be so careful about his manners and could have a third piece of cake without being told that 'young gentlemen never took more than two pieces.' The single aunt used to distribute religious tracts and sometimes she took Percy with her on these well-meant philanthropic expeditions. But the recipients of these endeavours to save their souls for a possible future life (in, Percy gathered, another world) did not always receive them in the spirit in which they were meant. Sometimes the door was shut with unnecessary force—an effective, if summary, dismissal. But if the religious tracts were accompanied by a pot of home-made jam or perhaps a small currant cake the welcome was a little warmer. On one occasion he was offered a cup of tea, but this was exceptional, for their reception was, as a rule, of the chilliest.

During several weeks of one term he was kept at home with a severe attack of rheumatic fever and spent part of his convalescence studying Latin. One day when the doctor called a Latin grammar and other books relative to the Latin language were lying on his counterpane. The doctor, with a slightly amused look on his face, asked Percy's mother if the study of Latin grammar was the boy's usual way of entertaining himself. But he really did like the study of languages, particularly French and Latin, and could get quite excited when poring over the appropriate dictionaries and grammars. He wanted to learn Greek but never got down to beginning the study of that language although he did buy a Greek dictionary, which he never made much use of.

In many cases the saying that the child is father of the man is true. In Percy Cane's case even from a very early age his sense of form that was to turn him into an eminent garden designer was developing. The way curtains hung, the arrangement of furniture in rooms, the placing of ornaments and other things—all these worried the boy if they did not seem to be just right.

And though it was to be some time before he really knew what he wanted to do for a career or what he was best fitted for, from very early days he was interested in architecture. But it was not the architecture of 'rows of small terraced houses, all more or less alike' that interested him, it was architecture in its wider applications. Why, for example, did old castles with massive wall spaces appear so fine? he asked himself. Why did what seemed to be too many windows or window spaces spoil the appearance of an architectural conception? Houses in which people had to pass their lives, he felt, must have plenty of light and air. Ideas such as these captured his imagination. Avidly he read books like *Modern Painters* in which the author, Ruskin (then still alive), insisted upon the superiority in landscape of the modern painters, especially of Turner, to that of the ancient masters. But it was from Ruskin's *The Stones of Venice* that he learned most about the foundations from which great architecture springs or should spring, and from other works of Ruskin such as *The Seven Lamps of Architecture, Lectures of Architecture and Painting, Elements of Painting,* and *Elements of Perspective.* Any books that threw light on works of art, paintings, and the works of Nature herself—the formation of clouds for example—all appealed strongly to the young Cane.

After leaving private school he studied for a time with a French tutor acquiring a 'passable' French pronunciation, as he put it, but which must have been fairly good for he managed for a time to run a small French class at home to get himself extra pocket-money.

He began to get restless, worrying about his future life and prospects. In spite of his fundamental, almost unconscious longing for a creative life, he felt he ought to do something practical—in other words he should earn his own living.

The name Crittall now comes into the story. And for any story connected with Braintree it can hardly be avoided for to this village, as it then was, came the ironmonger's son, Francis Crittall, who had hit upon the idea of metal windows after his mother had injured herself in raising a heavy wooden one. He brought out a steel window, which sold well not only because it was lighter than a wooden one, but when it was realised that these metal windows would not expand in tropical heat and also could not be eaten by white ants, a large trade was built up with countries such as India.

Francis Crittall's eldest son—who later became Sir Valentine Crittall—was at school with Cane but it was the younger son, Dick, who was an intimate friend. It was to Dick Crittall that he turned in 1903 in an endeavour to find himself useful, practical work to do and was given a job at the Crittall factory. Here he did not find things altogether to his liking: everything was new and strange. But this was to be expected. He got on well with his fellow workers but found that he did not have a great deal of interest in machinery—and this formed an essential part of life at Crittalls. He joined the firm on 14 February 1903 at a wage of 15s. a week. In April of that year it was increased to £1 and it continued to rise by small increments until when he left in January 1908 he was earning £2 a week, quite a fair wage in those days. After his quiet upbringing he found life at the factory rather rough and raw. Such events as staff outings, for example, were never very much liked by him. On one occasion the outing was to Yarmouth and his fellow-workers visited—it seemed to him—just about every pub in Yarmouth, and not content with that, took a barrel of beer on board the coach for the return journey. It is easy to see that the young Cane was not too happy in these circumstances and though all his life he was in principle to be a total abstainer from alcohol he did find it necessary at certain times during his stay at Crittalls to take a few sips of brandy from a flask to keep him going whenever the work was more tiring than usual. But the years he spent at Crittalls gave him an insight into human relations and business which he was never to lose.

Meanwhile he had not been entirely neglecting his artistic inclinations. In fact he was lapping up anything to do with the artistic activities of life 'like a starving cat placed in front of a saucer of milk.' He learned to draw and appreciate art. Having begun lessons on the piano at the age of seven (he was to be over seventy when he had his last lesson) he industriously practised scales and exercises at the early hour of 6.30 a.m., much to the discomfort of his parents whose bedroom was directly above, until he had saved enough money to buy a small upright piano (a Bechstein) which he installed in the morning-room at the bottom of the hall where he was able to play to his heart's content without disturbing anyone. He next bought a violin but after a few lessons reluctantly came to the conclusion that his ear was not good enough. He began learning the organ which gave him a lot of pleasure, but he found that piano and organ together were rather too much to cope with and so decided to concentrate on the piano which had the advantage of not needing a blower. But he was proficient enough to play the organ at a local church and continued doing this until one afternoon he had to accompany a member of the church in a rendering of a popular song. The man not only could not sing well but completely ignored the bars which should have been rests. 'I did my best to keep up with him,' said Percy, 'but it was a difficult contest, and I came in a few bars behind at the end.' This encounter finished Percy as a public performer on the organ. Another of his artistic endeavours was painting but this he found took up too much time so he renounced it in favour of the piano.

More important than any of this, however, was his decision to attend art school. He enrolled at the Chelmsford College of Science and Art (later the Mid-Essex Technical College). And just as his time at Crittalls gave him an insight into business activities and human relations, so his time at this art school gave him a heightened appreciation of works of art. He still did not know what he really wanted to do with his life but in a semi-conscious way he knew he wanted to do something unusual. He needed an aim in life and, having recognised that aim, he wanted the opportunity of working for its fulfilment. His thoughts turned to gardening of which he had always been fond. After he had been at the art school for a while and had become quite proficient in drawing and designing he began helping friends of the family with the lay-out of their gardens which in general he thought were rather unimaginative.

One day at the art school the principal (C. H. Baskett, A.R.A.) noticed one of these gardening sketches and asked Cane to bring some to show the examiners who were coming to the school the following day. Cane willingly agreed and next day brought designs and sketches and spread them around to make them look as impressive as possible. The examiners came and as they paused to look at Cane's work, the principal remarked that the pupils were there to learn to design. Cane, with all the conceit of his young years, broke in with 'No one ever taught me to design: that was born in me.' As soon as he had said it he would have given anything to have recalled the remark for the principal had taken a real interest in him and his work. A chilly silence followed. Cane felt that feelings between him and the principal were never quite the same again. In fact, soon afterwards the principal told him that he felt that he, Cane, had learnt all he could at the art school and offered him an introduction to the secretary of the Architectural Association in London so that he could study architecture full-time. But Cane by this time had made quite a number of local connections by designing gardens in the Chelmsford district and decided he could not afford to give all his time to the study of architecture: he did contact the secretary, though, who suggested that he might like to study part-time and, this proposal being accepted, arranged for him to be a pupil of one of the senior students whose name was Stephen Rowland Pierce; he proved to be a very good coach.

(Pierce, who won the Rome scholarship, later went into partnership with C. H. James and was partly responsible for the Norwich City Hall and the town hall at Slough. He had a rather difficult temperament and not much patience under opposition although plenty in his work. He died in 1966.)

But what proved to be the crucial turning point in Cane's life—the point when he finally realised that what he wanted to be was a garden architect—was a visit to Easton Lodge, the seat of the Countess of Warwick, near Dunmow in Essex. Easton Lodge, known since Norman times, had changed hands frequently until the end of the sixteenth century when it became the property of the crown and was granted by Queen Elizabeth I to Sir Henry Maynard. In the nineteenth century it came into the hands of the Countess of Warwick who was very interested in gardening. Among her many activities in this sphere was the founding of a college for women gardeners which became the well-known Studley Horticultural College. The Countess transformed the gardens at Easton Lodge, the work being carried out under the superintendence of the garden architect, H. A. Peto.

When Cane visited Easton Lodge it had just been altered and was a talking point in gardening circles. The house stood on gradually rising ground and, though rather exposed, had an 800-acre park to give protection. Three wide avenues converged through the park on to the house. According to a report by H. Avray Tipping in *Country Life* of 23 November 1907, which describes the gardens very much as Cane must have seen them:

Easton was, five years ago, deplorably deficient in pleasant garden surroundings, those in existence consisting of the very moderate-sized square of grass, cut up with a rather commonplace flower-bed arrangement . . . Beyond that was an uncompromising croquet-ground bounded by the iron rail of the park. As, owing to road and right of way to the south, the garden was to the north, it had the added dreariness of being swept by the north-east blast, and when, in 1902, the new garden works were instituted, it was rightly decided to prefer shelter to extended outlook towards the north, while the south views, which . . . we must consider the best, remained unimpeded.

A considerable slice of park, which at this point was flat and featureless, was enclosed, and form and definiteness were given to the croquet-ground by stretching down each side of it the fine pergolas of sixteenth-century type, with their pillared supports and round, arched roofs centring in domes, already wreathed and bowered with creepers; while beyond this much improved old section of the garden was constructed the ample and dignified sunk garden . . . that best of all materials Ham Hill stone being used for the purpose.

The central feature of this garden is a balustered pool, akin to the original one at Montacute but on a larger scale, as it takes the form of a canal over 100 ft. in length, which in summer is literally ablaze with various coloured water-lilies. . . . the ample stretch of paving is reached by six flights of steps, while around and above the great sunk square run broad grass terraces, sentinelled with Irish yews, bounded by cypress hedges and terminated by semi-circular classic seats. From both ends of the sunk garden open shrubberies with wide grassy ways and intelligently set with groups and masses of choice and varied flowering bushes that give a long succession of interest and variety of colour in blossom, leaf and twig, for the planting has been carried out with a view to autumn tints, so that late in the year the garden is almost as lovely and interesting as in the earlier seasons. But these shrubberies do not match, for the western one merges into a different and ungeometrical feature. Access was here desirable to a long natural fold or concavity in the otherwise plain slope of the park and in order that this access might be both sheltered and picturesque a gradually descending valley was excavated, the earth so obtained being thrown up in haphazard banks and mounds on either side and a very considerable effect of depth thus given to the artificial hollow. This hollow has been made to resemble the natural valley which it joins and forms part of, while occasional rocks cropping up amid junipers and heaths complete a very agreeable stretch of wild gardening. The hollow eventually reaches some old fish-ponds, into one of which has been built on piles a charming Japanese tea-house . . . while on the pond margins are groups of a wise selection of water-loving plants. About seventy Salvation Army waifs were employed in addition to the available local labour . . . and Mr. Peto collected the many antique vases, urns, columns and statues which lend such point and distinction to this well-imagined and wholly successful example of modern garden making.

'This well-imagined and wholly successful example of modern garden making' made an impression on the young Cane that was to stay with him all his life. It certainly made him decide that this was what he wanted to do—to take an old, perhaps ugly, garden and transform it into a thing of beauty and pleasure. So it can perhaps be said that Henry Ainsworth Peto, the designer of Easton Lodge, had the first positive influence on Cane. Peto was a practising architect who modelled many of his gardens on the old Italian ones. Normally designed in the classical style, his gardens were well embellished with judiciously chosen trees, shrubs and plants and ornamented with statuary and other architectural features.

Around this time Cane met Geoffrey Holme the editor of *The Studio* art magazine and from this introduction developed a friendship which lasted many years until Holme went to America. Geoffrey Holme was brilliantly clever in his own art world and in his kind, almost unobtrusive way did a great deal to extend Cane's rather limited knowledge of painting and indeed of art in all its many forms. Delightful weekends were spent at Holme's house, an old rectory near Witham in Essex, where on the principal landing the bedroom doors had been painted in a series of different colours—a kind of chromatic scale of colour. Later Holme was to publish some of Cane's designs in *The Studio* and help him to become more widely known as a garden architect.

Cane also met the owner of a monthly garden periodical, *My Garden, Illustrated*. This was Bernard Martin, a large-scale farmer at Headbourne Worthy near Winchester in Hampshire and the owner of racing stables in Ireland. His wife Kathleen was the horticulturist of the two and she was very fond of her garden. In her impetuous Irish way she one day telephoned Cane to say that she and her husband were going abroad for a while and to ask whether Cane would like to come and alter anything in their garden that he felt needed changing. Cane, in youthful enthusiasm, promptly altered half the entire garden and then was dreadfully worried as to whether the alterations would be found acceptable. On her return Kathleen Martin telephoned Cane, but, perhaps deliberately, did not mention the garden. Cane was forced to ask her outright what she thought of it. The answer was typically Irish—she didn't know whether she liked the alterations or not; but she did know that the other half must be similarly altered the following autumn.

My Garden, Illustrated, edited first by Geoffrey H. Henslow, had begun publication in July 1914 as a magazine 'devoted to the interest of all who love and enjoy a garden as a relaxation from other pursuits.' It cost 6d. an issue, and was on art paper with colour plates. Donald McDonald, author of several books on gardening and agriculture, and a relative of Cane's on his mother's side, took over as editor in May 1915, 'after an exhaustive enquiry which convinces me that this high class monthly journal has come to stay, notwithstanding the strenuous times.' At McDonald's suggestion Cane sent plans, designs and sketches for gardens. These were accepted and he was asked for more. Cane was delighted and though the remuneration was 'not excessive' it was all welcome publicity for the budding garden architect. Cane's first article appeared in June 1915, entitled 'A Bungalow Garden.' Two further articles that year were on 'Herbaceous Borders' and 'Fruit Garden and Wild Garden.' With a war on it must have been a trying time to bring out a magazine but McDonald persevered. In January 1916 he wrote in an editorial:

> May the present year prove more encouraging to garden beauty than its cheerless and warstained predecessor . . . In spite of disturbances, political or otherwise, which may agitate the surface of national life, the spring, summer and autumn will come as usual, bringing their productions with them. Gardening gives no small contribution to national prosperity, and it has been well said that one of the greatest evidences of our progress is the growth of horticulture . . .

By now Cane was writing full-length articles accompanied by excellent pen and ink drawings done by himself.

Restrictions of the war gradually increased though in October 1916 Cane could still write (in an article on bungalow gardens):

> Through the effects of the war on the available supply of labour and in other ways, it may be advantageous at the present time, at all events

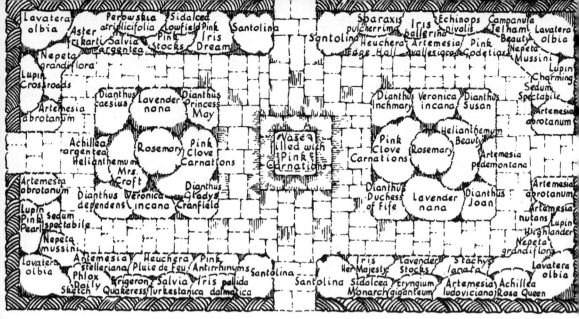

Formal planting varieties in silver, grey, pink and lavender in the 1930s

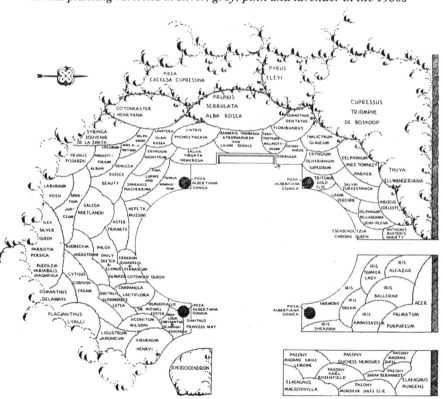

Planting scheme terminating an extended vista, 1937

Opposite, top: Colour grouping for herbaceous border in the 1930s
Opposite, bottom: A double border in shades of yellow, orange and blue.
Varieties of flowers available in the 1930s

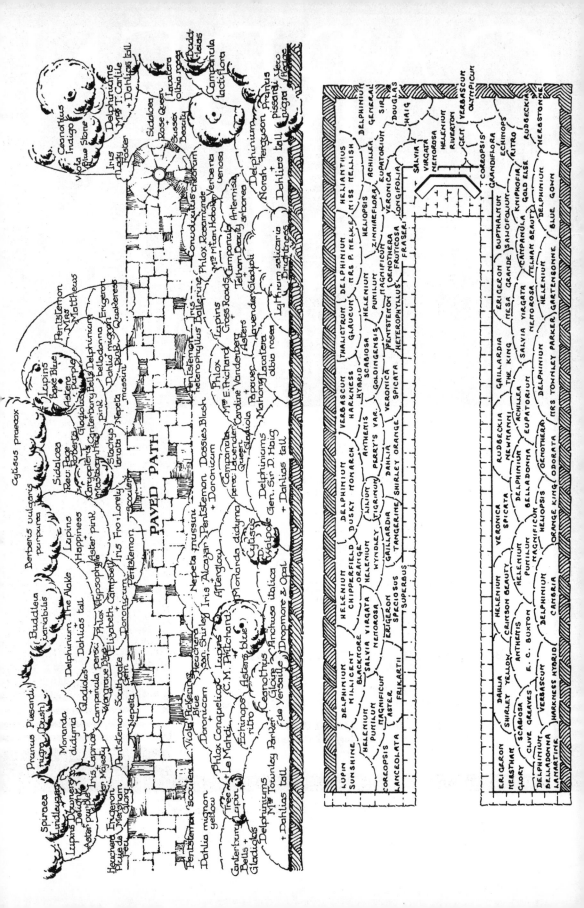

GARDEN DESIGN

A Quarterly Journal of
Horticulture & Garden Architecture

Contents

PRICE ONE SHILLING

No. 28 · WINTER 1936

Percy Cane's own journal, Garden Design

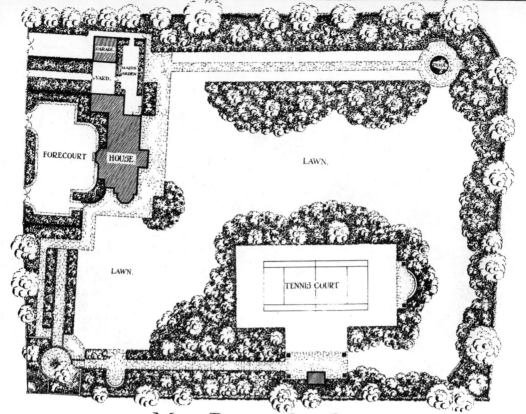

Mr. Percy S. Cane
Garden Architect

invites enquiries in connection with all matters relating to gardens, the development of estates, public parks, and recreation grounds.

Designs prepared and professional advice given.

Construction work and planting carried out by expert foremen under personal supervision.

Particulars of charges for preparing plans and carrying out the work will be forwarded upon application.

12, Cliveden Place, Eaton Square, S.W.1
Telephone : Sloane 3225

Business advertisement in the 1930s

Radiating stone paving with brick borders

Variation and pattern in paving

Victorian house—before

Victorian house—after

Pattern for a brick path

A pool-garden and pergola

A paved courtyard

Formal garden with glade leading off

A terrace with steps to a lawn

Opposite, top: A circular paved court bounded by stone walls
Opposite, bottom: Pool-garden with a fine tree on its long axis

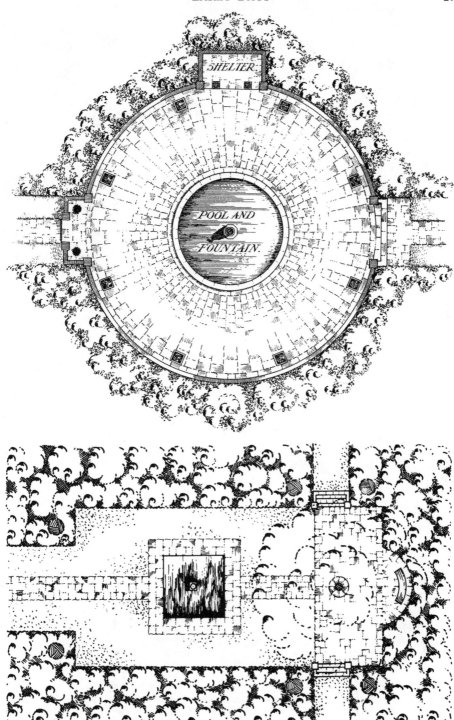

A good placing for garden shelters

Opposite, top: Corner treatment as a setting for an octagonal shelter
Opposite, bottom: An effective setting for a garden shelter

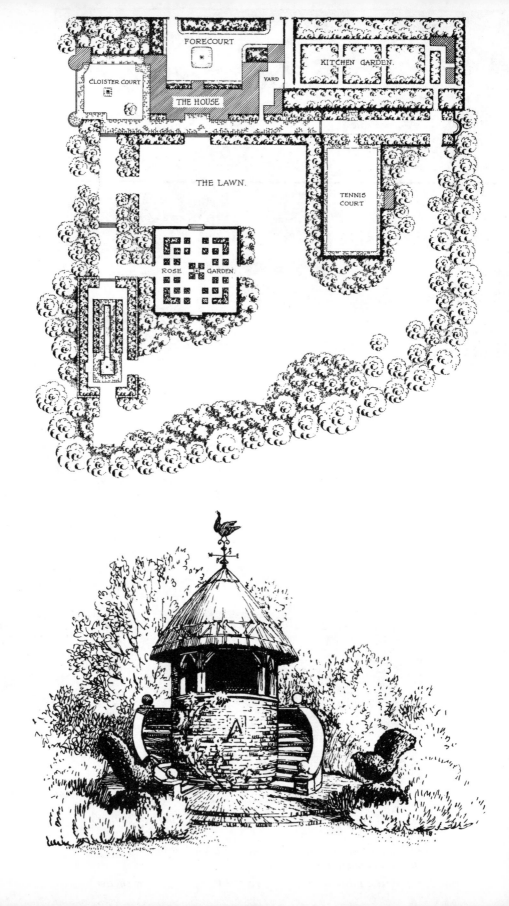

FORECOURT

KITCHEN GARDEN.

CLOISTER COURT

YARD

THE HOUSE

THE LAWN.

TENNIS COURT

ROSE GARDEN.

Brick steps and path leading to a terrace and garden door

Opposite, top: Plan for a five-acre garden
Opposite, bottom: A garden look-out among trees

Pool-garden and stairway

Opposite, top: Lavender or herb garden
Opposite, bottom: Tennis pavilion

Garden Design

By PERCY S. CANE

THE ROSE GARDEN

during the summer months, to live entirely at the seaside bungalow or country cottage, rather than follow the more usual custom of making it a place for visits as opportunity occurs.

The war caught up with Cane who was soon 'doing his bit' in the Food Production Department of the Board of Agriculture in Victoria Street. The next article by him in *My Garden, Illustrated* was published in August 1917 by which time the magazine had had to cut down on its editorial pages. The article was bylined 'By Percy Cane FRHS of the Food Production Department, Board of Agriculture' and was, of all things, on the spraying of potatoes. It was good war propaganda material, starting: 'No work in the garden can, at the present time, be of greater importance than the care bestowed on the potato, as a plentiful supply of the tubers will go far to lessen the consumption of bread.'

No September and October issues appeared but the next two dated November 1917 and March 1918 respectively contained articles by Cane on planning and planting the kitchen-garden and allotment (again using material inspired by the Board of Agriculture). The issue for May 1918 (Volume VIII No. 46) came out proudly headed 'Edited by Percy Cane.' It also contained the issue for June 'because of difficulty in obtaining paper.' It had few signed articles and from the style it would seem that Cane wrote most of them. By now he had left the Food Production Department of the Board of Agriculture so he was able to concentrate more on his journalistic work. The offer to become editor had reached him in a letter from Bernard Martin letting him know that McDonald was resigning. Would he like to take on the job? He was aware that he was not fully qualified but it was not an opportunity to be ignored. So he went for an interview, was offered the post and returned home 'metaphorically treading on air.'

In the July/August issue came an editorial 'Reconstruction and Country Life':

Gone is the old order of things never to return and a new one has to be built. A programme of reconstruction has to be formulated, making for its main objects, the re-population of the country districts; so far as is possible the production of sufficient food to make the nation self-supporting in this respect: and the transference of industries, of social activities, and, as far as may be, of all that goes to the enrichment of human life, from cities to the country.

It continued:

The future is pregnant with possibilities and calls for great men to grasp in their fullness, and deal greatly with tremendous issues. The Prime Minister, with far-seeing vision, has called for the erection of a new national life, to arise from wide reforms, having for their object the creating of conditions conducive to the fullest and happiest life possible for every member of the community . . .

The Prime Minister mentioned was Lloyd George and in another part of the magazine Cane printed Lloyd George's appeal to women to help bring in the harvest, which began:

The fields are ripening for the sickle; the toil of the winter and the spring is earning its reward. This is no ordinary harvest; in it is centred the hope and faith of our soldiers that their own heroic struggle will not be in vain.

It was a difficult period for a garden magazine, especially one dealing with the ornamental side of horticulture, and the owner Bernard Martin eventually decided he could carry it on no longer. He offered it to Cane who thereupon became owner as well as editor.

Having taken on this additional responsibility Cane decided that if he was to be a knowledgeable and responsible editor it was necessary to know more about the fundamentals of horticulture. To get this knowledge he enrolled at the Chelmsford County School of Horticulture. The horticultural instructor was C. T. Wakeley who had come to Chelmsford from Kew Gardens and was widely known as an authority. (The School of Horticulture later changed its name to the East Anglian Institute of Agriculture and finally to the Essex Institute of Agriculture with headquarters at Writtle.) The one event of this period of training in horticulture which stayed with Cane for the rest of his life was that someone stole his new bicycle one lunch-time and he never got it back!

Cane made great efforts to keep *My Garden, Illustrated* going. The February/March issue of 1919 stated that

. . . commencing with the April issue *My Garden* will appear in an enlarged form, and will, while still maintaining its unique standing as a periodical treating of horticulture alike for the extensive grounds of the mansion and for smaller gardens, will deal with subjects of a wider range of interests: its pages will deal with domestic and garden architecture and garden making for small and large gardens . . . it will deal with the problems of reconstruction.

   After the strain, for many people, of four years of nigh incessant over-work and anxiety and for those returning from scenes the horror of which can only be imagined by those who have not seen them, the relaxation of gardening and practice of horticulture in some of its many forms comes as a positive release.

The next number seems to have been for July and it was labelled Volume IX (New Series), the April issue having been Volume VII. It was now priced at one shilling instead of sixpence and had returned to colour printing which had been a casualty of the war. Its title was enlarged to *My Garden, Illustrated, the House and Estate.* Cane was still contributing many articles himself. One on village planting proclaimed that

   . . . the utmost attention should be given to the design and grouping of the number of new houses built to supply the urgent needs of workers and many other people . . . villages of the future must be centres of life amidst beautiful surroundings.

   Other contributors were coming back and a new department was started 'under the control of our Editor Mr. Percy Cane for the assistance of our subscribers in their gardening difficulties and doubts'. So what Cane had learnt at the School of Horticulture was being used to good effect.

   And in that issue of July 1919 there appeared a small advertisement for the first time:

PERCY S. CANE
LANDSCAPE AND GARDEN ARCHITECT
6, BOUVERIE STREET, FLEET STREET,
E.C. 4

Cane was at last in business as a garden architect. During the next two years the magazine changed its address twice and Cane's advertisement carried these new addresses. He was working from his office to a great extent though he still had a home in Essex. June 1920 seems to have been the date of the last copy of *My Garden, Illustrated* to appear and in this Cane had an advertisement saying that he was operating from '67 & 68 Broad Street Avenue and at Chelmsford'.

   War over, Cane took up garden architecture as a full-time profession.

He was beginning to realise its full potential: until then, his notions of garden design had been rather limited; the words 'garden design' conjured up pictures of being taken round friends' gardens, ending as likely as not with a tour of the kitchen-gardens to admire all the fruit and vegetables! Suddenly the chrysalis stage was over and the work developed into something greater than he had ever dreamt of.

2
The Making of a Garden Architect

A strange thing about Percy Cane was that although he was to rise to eminence as a garden architect he had no specific training in designing gardens. But as we have seen he had a thorough grounding in art and in horticulture, two essentials for such a profession.

He loved designing: in fact he loved creative work of any kind. He had natural good taste. For example, one day at Hascombe Court, the then residence of Sir John Jarvis at Godalming in Surrey, his hostess Lady Jarvis asked him his advice on the arrangement of furniture in her drawing-room. Something did not seem quite right to her, she said, but she did not know what. Cane realised at a glance that there was too much furniture in the room so that it was not possible to see the separate pieces clearly enough to appreciate them. He suggested moving a few things out and when this arrangement was to his satisfaction he stood in the doorway with Lady Jarvis and together they surveyed his work.

'Yes', said Lady Jarvis, 'it certainly looks better . . . but the trouble is you have thrown out all the pieces my husband likes best'. But she went on, 'Sir John does what *he* likes in the garden but he does allow me a little liberty indoors. So we'll leave it'.

At another time he was staying at the home of Herman Lebus at Hatley Park in Bedfordshire. Lebus liked to take Cane round the gardens by moonlight after dinner or early on a Sunday morning. On one such Sunday, Cane went downstairs before any of the family were about and had the temerity to criticise the arrangement of flowers in the staircase hall. The head gardener who had arranged them complained of lack of suitable flowers. Cane said, 'Come with me', and knowing the gardens almost as well as the head gardener took him to the kitchen garden where he cut some handsome heads of rhubarb flowers with long stalks. These, with some equally long branches of young foliage, he arranged loosely in large glass vases. They looked superb. He was afraid he had annoyed the head gardener but nothing was said.

What else then did go to the making of this eminent garden architect? What and who were the main influences on his work?

A brief review of gardening in England will put Cane's work into perspective. The earliest gardens in Britain were mostly those of monasteries—generally formal plots surrounded by high walls as exemplified in the present-day College Garden at Westminster Abbey. Vegetables and herbs were mostly grown to begin with: not until Elizabethan times did flowers become popular. When life became safer and castle gave way to mansion, the landscape of the grounds was given formal treatment with regular lines extending from the house into the surrounding domain. But the bounds of the garden were always clearly defined by high walls or hedges making a definite break between the garden and the surrounding country.

As the climate of the British Isles is suitable for growing a wide range of trees and plants, the pioneers soon developed a love of, and taste for, plants and gardens. And this love grew over the years. In the eighteenth century it evolved into what is known as the landscape school, a formal concept which lasted until about the middle of the century. This meant that the whole garden area was usually cut into square or rectangular plots separated by straight paths. These were often lined by trees whose branches were trained over them to form pleached alleys while evergreens like box and yew were formalised and planted to emphasise the design. Considerable use was made of water. The early flower-beds were simple in design not only in shape but in the way in which they were planted. The knotted beds which were a feature of Elizabethan times were made of twisting patterns worked out in dwarf evergreens such as lavender and box. Then came parterres in which motifs copied from embroidery and the like were reproduced in flowers and coloured earths. Various fashions also spread from the Continent. Holland provided a lavish use of topiary, lead statues, urns and bulbs; France encouraged a grand, formal style exemplified by Le Nôtre. From Italy came a revival of Palladian architecture, a classical style based on ancient Roman principles of design, to be followed by settings reminiscent of an Italian country landscape or, at any rate, the landscape idealized by the Italian painters of the period.

The 'country landscape' type of garden design resolved itself in Britain into the landscape idiom which came to be regarded as the national style of garden. Lancelot 'Capability' Brown was one of its chief exponents. In his hands many of the older gardens were altered out of all recognition. Hedges were swept away, hills rose up as if by magic, and water appeared where formerly there had been dry land. It was a complete revolt against the earliest, strictly formal gardening. A typical Brown design took out boundary lines and put in ha-has. Lawns started some distance away from the house giving an appearance of unbroken lawn or parkland and they usually sloped down to an informal stretch of water. The principal views were framed and accentuated by the grouping of trees to produce a number of vistas leading down to the water.

Humphrey Repton was a successor but he kept more of the past. Then came the Victorian age with many experiments in style, including a revival of formalism of the worst kind, using a profusion of garden ornaments. But in general certain factors remained constant: all gardens had lawns or grass plots of some kind, pools, generally a hedge, and, if of any size, garden ornaments. The lawnmower had been invented in 1831 (by Edwin Budding) and lawns were now more than ever the pride of English gardeners. A typical Victorian setting was a lawn stretching south from the drawing-room windows with tall specimen trees or shrubs dotted about. Near the house would be beds and borders with standard roses or filled with geraniums, lobelias and yellow calceolarias. There would be a large hedge of clipped yew or of laurel between the house and the lawn. There would be shrubberies on either side of the lawn, crowded with box, laurels, aucubas and other not particularly interesting shrubs and plants, with occasional large clumps of pampas grass. Through the shrubbery would be narrow paths with a rustic seat, and dahlias often stood primly in neatly staked rows. A walled garden produced the fruit and vegetables.

Bedding-out became a rage. In its heyday it was an unmistakable form of gardening. Flowers and foliage plants were used to obtain broad colour effects in regular patterns. Enormous numbers of plants, mostly annuals and biennials, many of them tender, were raised every year and set out in geometrical patterns. The plants had to be of the kind which would all be in full bloom together and have a long flowering period. Joseph Paxton, head gardener at Chatsworth House, is often given the credit (or blame) for introducing bedding-out. He started with it around 1830 and soon it was being imitated by most of the great houses of the country and also in thousands of smaller suburban gardens. But luckily the craze failed to infect the English cottage garden.

The revolt against this formalism was spearheaded by William Robinson who was able to express his ideas forcibly through his several magazines which included *Gardening, Gardening Illustrated, Cottage Gardening,* and *Flora and Sylva* and in his many books of which *The English Flower Garden* (published in 1883 and revised several times) is the best known. *The English Flower Garden* was a major landmark of Victorian gardening. In it Robinson says that gardeners had suffered for a long time at the hands of the decorative artist who, when applying designs to the garden, made many of them 'wrong in plan and hopeless for the life of plants'. It had begun with 'knots' and suchlike patterns, he said, but had more recently developed into 'bedding-out', 'carpet bedding' and 'mosaic culture' in which the beautiful forms of flowers 'were degraded to the level of crude colour to make a design and without reference to the natural form or beauty of the plants'.

He goes on:

. . . the modern garden is often no more interesting than an oilcloth pattern, because instead of beautiful form and colour we see emphasis given to pattern-work and plants robbed of all their grace . . . the first duty of all who care for the garden as a picture is to see these noble natural forms in every part of his life and nature, and once they see them they will never mistake decorative patterns for art and beauty in a garden . . .

One of the first things we have to do is to get a clear idea of the hollowness of much of the talk about 'styles' that forms a great part of what has been written in books about laying out gardens . . . there are only two styles: the one strait-laced, mechanical, with much wall and stone, with water-squirts, plaster-work and absurd sculpture; the other natural—in most cases, once free of the house accepting the ground lines of the earth herself as the best, and getting plant beauty from its natural source—the flowers and trees arranged in picturesque ways.

There are positions where stonework is necessary; but the beautiful terrace gardens are those that are built where the nature of the ground required them . . . there is no such thing as a style fitted for every situation; only one who knows and studies the ground well will ever make the best of a garden, and any 'style' may be right when the site fits it.

Treatment for the front of a small house

A corner seat forming a striking turning point in a small garden

Recessed pool at the end of a paved walk

A simple scheme for a small building plot

ROSE GARDEN PLANTING PLAN—REFERENCE TO BEDS:—

1. Mrs. Henry Morse. 2. Picture. 3. Mrs. H. Bowles. 4. W. E. Chaplin. 5. McGredy's Scarlet. 6. Mrs. Sam McGredy. 7. Duchess of Atholl. 8. Polly. 9. Christine. 10. Lady Forteviot. 11. Mrs. G. A. Van Rossem. 12. Southport. 13. Portadown. 14. Rapture. 15. Dame Edith Helen. 16. Betty Uprichard. 17. Etoile de Hollande.

A selection of rose varieties for 1936

A sunken pool-garden

A small town garden

A plan for a one-and-a-half-acre garden

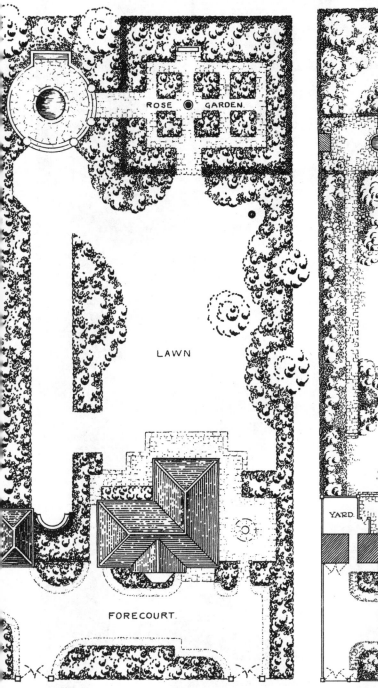

A plan for a half-acre garden

Town garden

· A · GARDEN ·
of
· 1½ · ACRES ·
PERCY · S · CANE

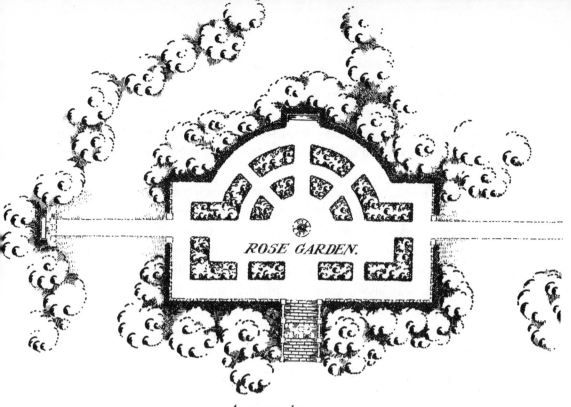

A rose-garden

Three-quarter-acre garden

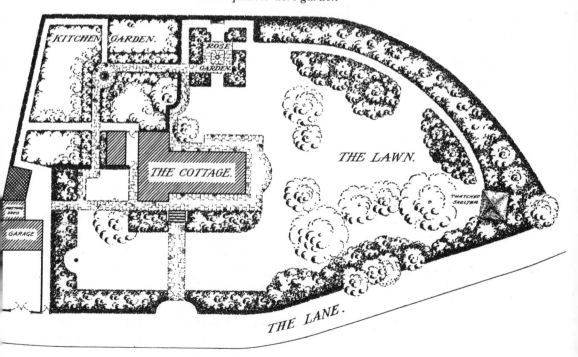

Opposite: A garden of one-and-a-half acres

Robinson denounced every aspect of formalism but he came up against bitter criticism from many leading architects of the time. He worked at a period when the host of self-reliant shrubs and plants from Western China were on their way and new gardens for a wealthy suburban population were being asked for.

Gertrude Jekyll, an educated, artistic, much travelled lady, came into Robinson's life in about 1875. Proficient in several crafts, she began designing gardens in which woodland and water were treated naturally in the Robinsonian manner. She pioneered the herbaceous border and developed the use of stone walls for a mass display of rock and alpine plants. She was also a specialist in rock and water plants. She had an artist's sense of colour and of planting for colour effect. She also had the knowledge to select the best plants from the large number by then available.

Of course there were challengers. Reginald Blomfield, for example, in his *The Formal Garden in England* attempted to separate garden design from horticulture; he wanted the designing to be done by a professional architect to some traditional pattern and the horticultural side to be subservient to the architectural. John Dando Sedding, a trained architect, published *Garden-Craft Old and New* in 1891 and this, too, emphasised the importance of the architectural side of making gardens. Sedding died before his book was published but a preface written by him from The Croft, West Wickham in Kent in 1890 reads:

> The old-fashioned garden, whatever its failings. in the eyes of the modern landscape-gardener (great is the poverty of his invention) represents one of the pleasures of England, one of the charms of that quiet, beautiful life of bygone times that I, for one, would fain see revived. And judged even as pieces of handicraft, apart from their poetic interest, these gardens are worthy of careful study. They embody ideas of ancient worth; they evidence fine aims and heroic efforts; they exemplify traditions that are the net result of a long probation. Better still, they render into tangible shapes old moods of mind that English landscape has inspired; they testify to old devotion to the scenery of our native land, and illustrate-old attempts to idealise its pleasant traits.
>
> Because the old gardens are what they are—beautiful yesterday, beautiful today, and beautiful always—we do well to turn to them, not to copy their exact lines, nor to limit ourselves to the range of their

ornament and effects, but to glean hints for our garden enterprise today, to drink of their spirit, to gain impulsion from them. As often as not, the forgotten field proves the richest of pasture.

He goes on to talk of the supposed harm that Kent and Brown had done.

So began the rage of making all the surroundings of a house assume a supposed appearance of rude Nature. Levelling, ploughing, stubbing-up, was the order of the day. The British navvy was in great request—in fact the day that Kent and Brown discovered England was this worthy's natal day. Artificial gardens must be demolished as impostures, and wriggling walks and turf put where they had stood. Avenues must be cut down or disregarded; the groves, the alleys, the formal beds, the terraces, the balustrades, the clipped hedges must be swept away as things intolerable. For the 'landscape style' does not countenance a straight line, or terrace, or architectural form, or symmetrical beds about the house; for to allow these would not be to photograph Nature. As carried into practice the style demands that the house shall rise abruptly from the grass, and the general surface of the ground shall be characterised by smoothness and bareness.

William Robinson's point of view on landscape gardening broadened a little as time went on until it was much like that of the poet and artist William Morris, who wrote in *Hopes and Fears for Art*, 'Large or small, the garden should look both orderly and rich. It should be well fenced from the outside world. It should by no means imitate either the wilfulness or the wildness of Nature, but should look a thing never seen except near a house.'

Another man to make his mark on garden design, who made a deep study of it and was particularly fond of the old Italian gardens, was Sir George Sitwell. In the preface to his book, *An Essay on the Making of Gardens*, published in 1909 with the subtitle 'A Study of Old Italian Gardens, of the Nature of Beauty, and the Principles involved in Garden Design,' he says that the revival of 'the newly recovered art of garden design' owed much to English architects and he singles out Sedding, Blomfield, and Thomas. But he felt that the formal garden in England still fell short of the great examples of the Italian Renaissance for it was seldom related as it should be to the surrounding scenery, was often wanting in repose and nearly always wanted in imagination. 'If the world is to make great gardens again,' he says, 'we must both discover and apply in the changed circumstances of modern life the principles which guided the garden-makers of the Renaissance, and must be ready to learn all that science can teach us concerning the laws of artistic presentment.'

Harold Ainsworth Peto, whom we have met in the previous chapter as the designer of Easton Lodge, the garden of which made Cane turn to garden designing as a career, was a formalist. He had his own lovely garden at Ilford Manor, Bradford-on-Avon: another he designed is at Wayford Manor in Somerset.

Sir Edwin Lutyens, a distinguished architect, took a great interest in gardens and for their layout he often sought the co-operation of his neighbour Gertrude Jekyll. Lutyens had a deep understanding of traditional craftsmanship and materials and when Miss Jekyll built her own house at Munstead Wood, Lutyens was the designer, and the formalist architecture of Lutyens combined with the naturalistic garden of Miss Jekyll was a combination which had a great influence on the design of gardening. Lutyens tended to look to the past, Miss Jekyll to the future; and in spite of her devotion to the principle of the cottage garden she employed new materials and new colours in a new manner well suited to the growing English need for labour-saving gardens.

Another associated with this movement of moderate formalism round a house built in the traditional manner and of traditional materials—or preferably an old house itself—was Nathaniel Lloyd. His own house, Great Dixter in Sussex, shows what he could achieve.

The work of these garden architects would have been known to Cane through books, by visiting the gardens they had designed or by reading the gardening press which began to proliferate towards the end of the nineteenth century. The *Gardeners Chronicle* founded in 1841 by Joseph Paxton continued to a great extent to uphold the older formalism but *Country Life* which arrived in 1897 gave much attention to the larger gardens in their aesthetic, practical and historical aspects and stimulated a greater interest in design among the middle class who were now buying their moderate to large houses. *Amateur Gardening* which preceded *Country Life* by over a decade aimed at the steadily increasing class of new gardeners who employed little or no labour.

Much of Cane's inspiration, however, came from the older classical designers. Humphrey Repton, for example, propounded a simpler, bolder treatment than had formerly been the case and emphasised that fine landscape needed fine architecture if it were not to seem meaningless to human eyes. Cane realised from Repton the need for and the immense desirability of the correct relation of the two. Lancelot 'Capability' Brown was another strong influence. Brown seemed to Cane to make landscape grander. His extensive woods always seemed to fit into the landscape as if they belonged there and his stretches of pasture seemed to be art applied to nature in the boldest, firmest way so that it would be impossible to improve them. As an instance of this Cane says that he was once at the Bowood house of Lord Colum Crichton-Stuart. He was asked to have a look at the Capability Brown planting around part of the lake and after the tour was asked whether he thought anything was not right or should be altered. Cane replied that only one thing did not seem to fit in with the general scheme—three standard prunus trees. Lady Colum Crichton-Stuart who accompanied Cane on the tour smiled and turning to her husband said quietly 'The only trees *we* have planted.' Capability Brown was vindicated.

Cane was also influenced very much by the grandeur of classical architecture, particularly the architecture of Greece and Italy. Classical architecture, he maintained, used conservatively and in conjunction with the forest trees which are nowhere seen to greater advantage than in Britain, could be superb. He went several times to Italy and Greece. His first visit to Italy brought 'floods of light' to him, he said, and to see wherever one went 'squares of all shapes, each, as a rule with a church as a sort of accent to the space as a whole. To walk from street to street, from square to square, each different to the others and each replete with its one interest was, to my eyes, a revelation.' But the outside appearance of the streets and squares he found was but as the shell to the kernel as seen in the interiors of the churches and other public buildings. For it was inside that the greater wealth of painting and sculpture was to be found . . . 'not always of first rate quality but here and there, like a jewel in its setting of works of lesser quality some masterpiece of the painter's and sculptor's art would be revealed.'

Of Italian painting Cane felt that the ceiling of the Sistine Chapel was superb. And of sculpture, Michelangelo's David, 'standing, when I saw it, supreme in its glory, centrally facing one at the end of the first corridor of the Accademia in Florence.' And were not the unfinished works of Michelangelo which lined the walls of the corridor, he felt, the most suitable approach that could have been arranged to lead to the breathtaking David? Another sculpture which gave him great pleasure was the Dying Gaul in the Capitoline Museum in Rome, 'a work so supremely lovely and embodying so much of human suffering, that to me it reveals the work of ancient sculptors, if it is truly representative of the sculptor's art of ancient times, as something equalling, if not surpassing, many of the works of sculptors of later times.' Just to wander through the streets of Rome, Florence and Venice gave unforgettable experiences to Cane. All these things helped to form his taste.

He made a resolution early in life to know and study the finest works that had been wrought by man and was determined that, as far as possible, he would go and see the grandest scenery. He felt that if one filled one's memory to its fullest capacity with the best things this world had produced, one's creative work in gardens, as in any other field, would be equal in quality to that mental wealth. Partly because of expense, partly because of want of time, he was not able to do this as fully as he wished but his visits to Italy and Greece in particular helped him immensely to understand how the art of these countries had given legacies to the world of European painting and sculpture. Fine gardens were not, naturally, excluded from the artistic works he studied.

In truth his taste was already partly formed. From his earliest days, as we have seen, he loved the arts, particularly architecture and music. But with architecture he found he could only be serious as far as its aesthetic sides were concerned. As a young child staying at Conway in Wales he looked at Conway Castle and thought how much finer those buildings with great wall spaces broken by few windows appeared than did smaller buildings with walls broken by many small openings.

Though he was very fond of music he was not creative as far as musical composition was concerned in the same way as he could be creative with form and colour. He was taken to hear Caruso sing at Covent Garden and says the experience was a revelation and influenced his whole life. Though he did not have much money at the time he went again the next night even though he had to take an uncomfortable seat in the gallery. But a new door had opened to the art of living and life to him was never quite the same again. It affected his work as a garden architect in a way, for he found that, when he was uncertain of what he ought to do or suggest for a particular problem in a garden, if he listened to suitable music, say something from *The Ring* for a serious design or, if he wanted sheer beauty, some Mozart or perhaps an excerpt from Verdi's *Aida,* and just thought about the problem, it would solve itself without any effort on his part.

So scenery, taste and beautiful objects all contributed to the make-up of the developing garden designer, Cane. In one of his first writings, in *My Garden, Illustrated,* January 1916, he wrote:

Composition is one of the most essential things in the making of really beautiful pictures. A master artist will, even when copying from Nature, arrange his subjects as only a master can. He will, if necessary, bodily transfer features, large or small, to any position on his canvas that he may require them to occupy.

And so exquisitely adjusted often is his work that the slightest addition or rearrangement would mar the whole. So it is with our garden making; the bare ground is our canvas, and shrubs and trees, flowers and stones are the paints. It rests with the artist to create scenes of perfect beauty, or to obtain results of less charm. Every group of trees may in itself be a picture, and the beds and borders can give successions of beautiful forms, and of lovely combinations of colours. Indeed, the garden maker has advantages not possessed by the artist, for while the creation of the artist presents one scene only, the garden maker may have endless scenes, each one a perfect picture, or pictures, seen from different aspects. The completed whole may be one changing scene of loveliness, every part of it varying in colour and light with every hour of the day, and with every day of the year.

Later in the same article he deals with formal versus natural styles of garden design.

There are many beautiful examples of both, and while for some places formal seems the only right treatment others may possess possibilities which require to be developed in quite an opposite manner. One may not generalise. Each place calls for separate treatment. Each needs to be developed on its own lines, and there should be no rival claims of formal or landscape styles. We should see that we have the best only of whatever is most suited to the particular surroundings that are being dealt with.

A house is a man-made object and cannot be rightly placed in the midst of green fields. Speaking generally, a certain amount of formality around the residence is called for. Formal planning may then be extended farther into the grounds, or more natural treatment may be reverted to. Gardens also are man's work, and it is better to delight openly in this fact, and to see that we have the best work possible, rather than to descend to the trickery of creating falsely so-called natural features.

Present-day design might often emulate more closely the atmosphere of dignity and stateliness surrounding some of the fine examples that may be seen of Elizabethan and other old houses. There is richness and order in their every proportion, their courtyards and terraces awake visions of the gay and happy life of the period, and the materials of which they are composed, stone or brick, or whatever it may be, are become with the passing of time so softened and beautiful in outline and colouring as to delight all beholders. The specimens that may be seen of old planning show us generally good materials used for direct purposes, there was no thought of imitation, the use and fitness of things, the excellence of materials and of craftmanship constituting the beauty.

And he goes on:

If we contrast this with some of the work of the present day, surely it will keep us to purer taste in our houses and grounds. . . . It is easy to do without superfluous features; true beauty can be obtained from the simplest arrangement of walk, or lawn, or flowers, and better far to be satisfied with the severest simplicity than to admit one particle of over-ornamentation, sham, or falseness. And by this I am not saying one word against anything that contains real excellence of design or workmanship, whether it be in the planning and making of the actual grounds, or of any ornaments, or any subsidiary features placed therein.

Ten years later he was writing (*The Studio* 1926-7):

Whether it be the soft liveliness of some pastoral landscape, or the more dramatic quality of hills or mountains, fine scenery has a quality to which the mind of everyone responds to a greater or lesser degree. It makes an appeal to the emotions akin to that experienced when hearing good music or on beholding some idealised beauty of form, such as a masterpiece of statuary. The human mind is sensitive in a thousand different ways, but the strong appeal that gardens and garden scenery make is general, and to a very remarkable degree. Everyone acquires, consciously or unconsciously, a personal and individual taste; but critical taste in relation to the art of garden design is generally less cultivated than it is to that of most other types of artistic work. Why this is so, it is difficult to say, for garden design is as much an art as any kind of work must be that has for its object the creation of beauty. Gardens are always before our eyes, they are at certain times almost lived in, and our minds are influenced by them, as they must be by anything that is part of life's setting.

He continues:

It is possible to treat every sort of work with the care, taste and
inspiration which is something akin to genius. The quality of art is
progressive, and excellent as certain gardens may be of their kind, there
are some which are definitely of higher artistic rank than others.
Probably the highest form of garden design is that which merges into
what may be called the creation of landscape, possibly enhanced by the
presence and contrast of architecture or sculpture . . .

But garden planning, said Cane, was not merely the piecing together
of a number of different kinds of gardens, such as a flower-garden, a rock-
garden, a water-garden and so on, without the exercise of any great care as
to the harmonious relationship of parts with the whole, nor did it imply the
scattering of ornaments, without due regard to their suitability. Garden
design was not this. Rather it was

. . . firstly an appreciation of the possibilities offered by skilful
management of the contours of the ground, which can be some of the
loveliest things in a garden. It is the realisation of the atmosphere of the
place and the development of that atmosphere in the best way. It is the
inclusion of formal terraces and gardens suitable to the character of the
house, and the relation and contrast of these with beautifully balanced
glades and planting. It is the appreciation of every existing tree, or group
of trees, water, slopes, hollows and views, and the relating of the new
scheme to them in such a way that when completed it would seem that
nothing else had been possible. It is the harmonious relation of the
garden to the house, and of the gardens to the surrounding scenery. It is
the contrast of lawns and walks or gardens of soft shades with those of
strong colours. It is the careful choice and nice placing of enough
ornaments to give the necessary interest at certain defined points—but
never one too many. It is the weaving of all these into a unity, so that one
longs to work or rest in it, and appreciate its wonderful beauty. If the art
of gardening is raised to a higher level it will, in its development, give
pleasure in proportion to the more critical taste that is at the same time
its cause and effect.

Forty years later, Cane returned to the same subject in his book *The
Creative Art of Garden Design* (1967). His introduction says:

Designing gardens is an art, but as in painting, the man who knows
little about art but knows what he likes, enjoys a picture that observes
certain basic principles. As in all the arts there are periods of growth and

of changing fashion, but the principles remain constant. To make a beautiful garden the garden maker must know not only what he is doing, but also why he is doing it. And to make the complete unity of design so necessary if the results are to be good, the garden-maker must have a knowledge of the technique of garden design, and of gardening and arboriculture.

He must have a plan like the studies an artist draws, before he begins, for a garden is a picture that every year paints through the seasons, changing with the years as plants grow tall, but its main lines—its trees and larger shrubs—must stay and its success depends on how well they are grouped in the picture. If he starts in an haphazard way without a plan, the different parts that together make the whole garden will almost certainly be out of proportion.

. . . We have to think of the garden as a complete entity, which we can walk around, only a picture gallery that is alive and growing. In a small garden . . . we can have a single picture, but seen from, say, the windows, the entrance and from the panoramic view we can obtain when walking round it. We cannot, however, mix two pictures, two styles, blending, for instance, Constable's 'Hay Wain' with a Dutch interior by Rembrandt, or it will look a mess. In a larger garden we can have a succession of pictures, the divisions being their frames, or we can flow them from one to another by means of centre vistas carried through the different gardens. If this planning is done skilfully it will result in an effect of greater space; if done badly we can make a fairly large garden look tiny and shut in.

Cane more or less solved most of the problems incidental to his own work by himself. Quite early in his career, for instance, he was designing a garden for a client in a village only a few miles from his own home and he wanted to get round a sharp angular corner in a glade he was making. An ordinary curve seemed awkward, not at all right. Wondering what to do he suddenly thought of the angles in his arms and legs. They cut in. He tried it on the ground and it worked. After that he used the idea in countless ways and in countless variations and almost invariably obtained the result he wanted.

3
Among the Gardens

Editing of *My Garden, Illustrated* brought Cane to the notice of people who were in a position to become his customers in having gardens designed. One of the first to call on him in his office off Old Broad Street in the City was a Mrs. Dennis. Would he help her with her garden?

Cane was very pleased to do so. Sharnden, the house of Mr. and Mrs. Sam Dennis at Mayfield in Sussex, opened on to a raised paved terrace. From the terrace and from the windows on the south elevation were lovely views but no sign of any gardens. Cane soon saw the reason for this. A garden was not necessary here. The outlook was so good that it had to be kept as it was. But with a house of this size, and in the country, it was certainly necessary to have gardens somewhere. The answer was to make them to one side so that they did not obtrude upon the views from the house. A stairway was built down from the terrace to a flagged path which was laid at the same time. Here, the flagged path, bounded by low dwarf walls on both sides, gave an easy and attractive approach to an eminently suitable site. A formal paved flower-garden, a rose-garden and, separated from this latter by yew hedges on both sides of a turf alley, a lavender-garden provided an interesting succession. On the higher level a terrace, bounded by walls built to sitting height, and a lawn with a paved walk running centrally through it gave a sort of upper promenade from which it was possible to look down on the formal gardens below. These formal gardens opened onto an outer glade which was made, as it were, to enclose and at the same time complete the fairly extensive set of gardens. Just as an opera, a sonata or other musical composition must give a feeling of balance and completion, so in the case of this garden the feeling of completion was given by the outer glade: it offered a complete change in its form and in the nature of its planting. Its borders were filled with flowering and evergreen trees and shrubs.

Sharnden was Cane's most ambitious project so far but he was quite happy with what he achieved and he never had any doubts as to the design being right in the main. Designing these gardens at Mayfield continued over some considerable time and on his visits Cane often went down in the evening when, after dinner, Mr. and Mrs. Dennis and he would tour the gardens and discuss future plans. The following day Cane would carry on with the practical side of the business.

Not long after he had made this garden Cane was consulted about the treatment of the gardens at Llanerch Park in North Wales, the house of Captain and Mrs. W. Piers Jones.

The mansion was approached by a drive which followed the line of least resistance through an extensive deer park to the forecourt. But following this line meant that the drive had to curve at one place to avoid an overhanging bluff, and at another to avoid a group of trees too good to be destroyed, eventually arriving at the last fairly level stretch when the mansion came into view. To keep deer out of the forecourt and gardens (for deer can leap over quite high fencing) protective railings had had to be put up and even then there was one exceptionally athletic stag which jumped anything and eventually had to be shot. House, garage and attendant outbuildings stood on high ground overlooking the valley to the north with its river, a streak of reflecting silver, flowing quietly below.

Siting the house in this particular spot had undoubtedly been done because of the view. The Captain and his wife had their rooms on the second floor and from these rooms, themselves lovely, the view was magnificent. But as was often the case, the house needed suitable connections with the gardens and in order to effect this relationship an upper paved terrace was laid onto which the principal reception rooms opened and from it a flight of stairs sixty-two feet long was built to descend to a second terrace.

When the plans for this were shown to the Captain the only item he questioned was the length of the steps; however, he told Cane to do as he liked and after the steps had been built he acknowledged that they were just right. The second terrace was made into a long, formal paved flower-garden and from here, by way of a second flight of steps also sixty-two feet long, one descended to a third terrace with lawns and tennis-courts. These courts were not too far from the house and yet, partly owing to the descending levels, not too outstanding—yet slightly noticeable, for Cane considered tennis to be a sociable game whose white-attired players added life to any garden scene.

On the west side of the upper terrace, cloisters were built as part of the garden scheme and these, turning in at right angles, led into a loggia. Elms and beeches growing tall behind them furnished a green background which enhanced the effect of the Italianate cloisters and loggia. A pergola was built from north to south across a large kitchen garden, partly to connect two gardens and partly to provide the means of growing roses and other climbing plants in the way best calculated to show off their beauty. The pergola with piers of red brick to harmonise with the walls was proportionally wide, paved, and clothed with climbing roses, vines and clematis; this feature gave character to the kitchen-garden. A wide herbaceous border was made against one of the kitchen-garden walls and this gained much in effect because well away from the wall and border but making a separate unit of this part of the gardens was a little wood which was lovely in spring with carpets of anemones, narcissi and other bulbs. With the wood on one side and, later, the flower border rich with carefully arranged colour, a flagged walk running parallel with the wall and border brought one to the swimming pool garden. In this enclosure smoothly cut lawns sloped down to the pool, the water of which was kept heated—something very much appreciated in North Wales! And the final aid to enjoyment was a heated shelter with dressing rooms, a bar for drinks and plenty of room to recover from the effort of swimming. From the northern end of this pool-garden a long flight of steps went down to the stream which ran along the bottom of the valley and following this stream was a walk which came back to the house and terraces through a different part of the gardens.

During one of Cane's visits to Llanerch Park he was asked over to Bodnant to lunch with Lord Aberconway. An invitation from the President of the Royal Horticultural Society was to Cane in the nature of a royal command. At that time Lord Aberconway had just purchased an old mill, a building of some distinction, and had had it erected at the end of a formal water-garden. The famous gardens of Bodnant were in their infancy. Cane liked the position of the new mill and said so, but otherwise all he could recollect of the visit in after years was that lunch was served in an open-fronted loggia and, having left his overcoat in the house and being too

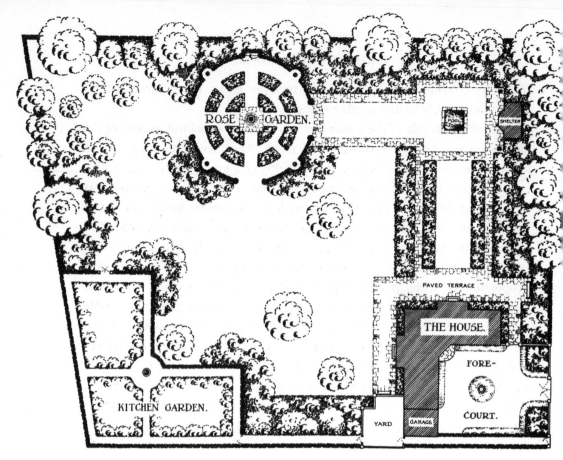

Three-acre garden

The gardens of Ardchoille, Frinton-on-Sea, Essex

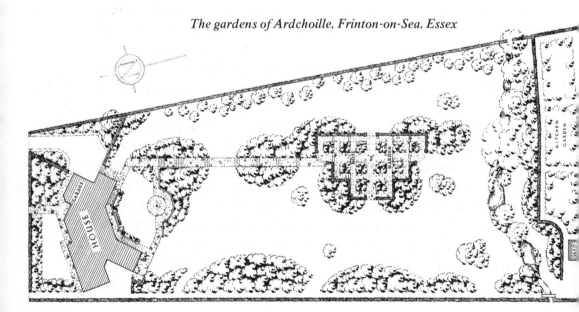

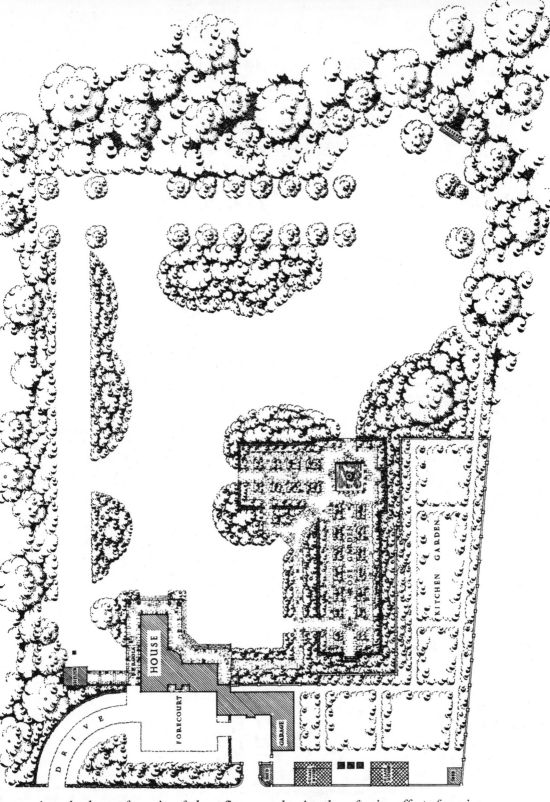

*A garden layout for a site of about five acres showing the softening effect of curving
borders on rectangular spaces*

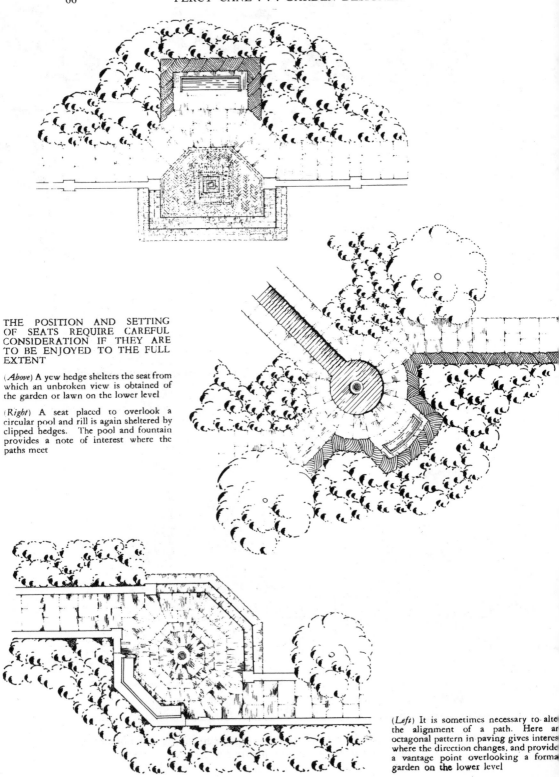

THE POSITION AND SETTING
OF SEATS REQUIRE CAREFUL
CONSIDERATION IF THEY ARE
TO BE ENJOYED TO THE FULL
EXTENT

(*Above*) A yew hedge shelters the seat from
which an unbroken view is obtained of
the garden or lawn on the lower level

(*Right*) A seat placed to overlook a
circular pool and rill is again sheltered by
clipped hedges. The pool and fountain
provides a note of interest where the
paths meet

(*Left*) It is sometimes necessary to alter
the alignment of a path. Here an
octagonal pattern in paving gives interest
where the direction changes, and provide
a vantage point overlooking a formal
garden on the lower level

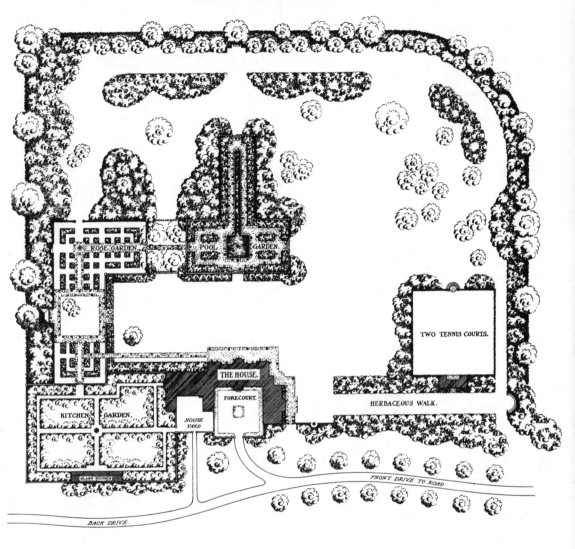

Plan for a gently sloping site of about fifteen acres

Opposite: The setting of seats

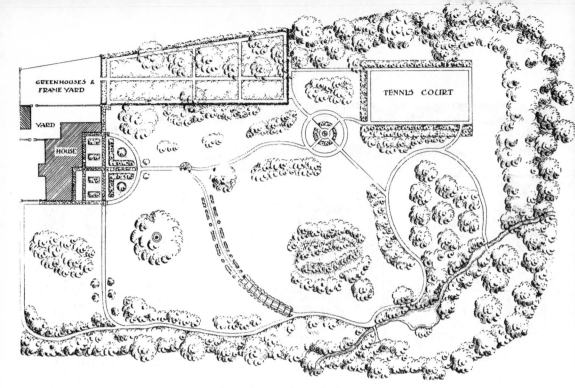

Victorian garden—before treatment

Victorian garden—after treatment

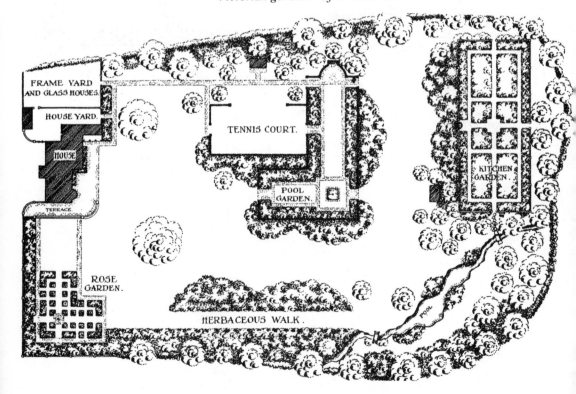

Opposite: Layout for a one-and-a-half-acre garden

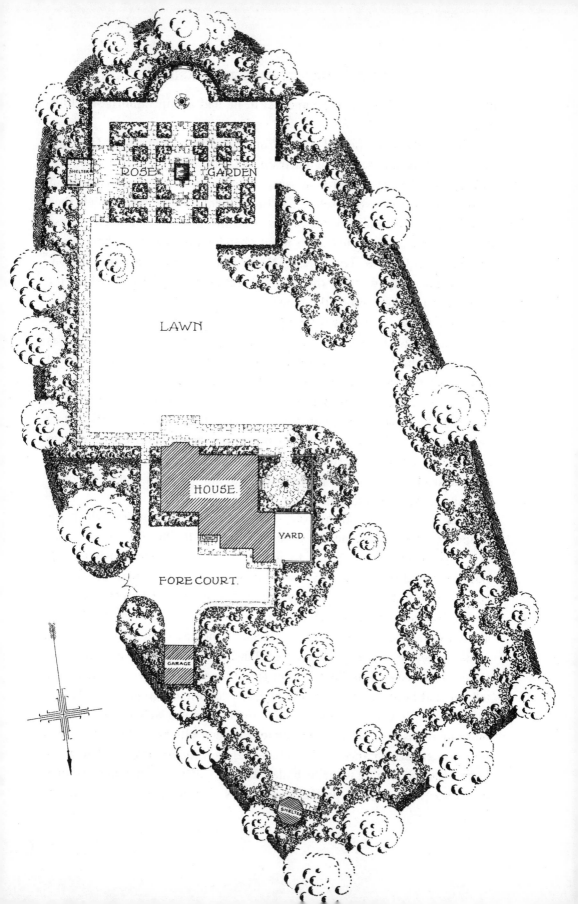

diffident to ask if he could go and get it, he had an uncomfortably chilly lunch!

Do creative activities all spring from the same root or roots? Does the act of painting landscapes or portraits, or indeed any form of painting, spring from the same source as, say, the composition or performance of good music? Is there some relation between them that, however widely they may diverge later, they are offsprings from the same parent stock? These thoughts came specially to Cane's mind when he was consulted about Anna Pavlova's gardens at Ivy House, North End, Hampstead in London. Pavlova not only wanted the gardens redesigned but also asked for balconies to be built on to the house.

Cane found it an interesting job. Pavlova was essentially an artist and like most artists she worked very hard, never counting the cost so long as she could improve her performance. As a result she rarely had any real spare time and as Cane was much in the same position they found it difficult to arrange appointments convenient to them both. Finally Pavlova suggested he might like to come to breakfast: Cane accepted and in fact went to several. They were excellent breakfasts: great silver dishes of eggs and bacon were handed round to a varied assortment of people who had come to see Pavlova. It was all very informal and pleasant and Cane found the talk interesting and stimulating.

Pavlova, who was always very enthusiastic about things in which she happened to be concerned, especially anything to do with creative art, would get excited and begin to gabble in Russian. Her husband, M. Dandre, would translate. As Cane did not speak a single word of Russian he was grateful for the translation, for at least it enabled him to follow the trend of the conversation. Pavlova at that time was giving a season of ballet at the Royal Opera House, Covent Garden. One day Cane told her he was going to see the performance on the following Monday. The next time she saw him she asked what he had thought of the performance and he had to tell her that because of a bad cold he had been unable to go. Pavlova said she was sorry to hear that and was glad to know he was well again. The next morning in his post he received a note from her with two tickets for a box for the next performance of 'Swan Lake.' He got the impression that 'Swan Lake' was Pavlova's favourite ballet. He also believed that her eventual death was due, at least partly, to overwork, for her artistic life was one unending struggle for perfection. She was very fond of exotic birds and to gratify this love the already quite spacious conservatory at Ivy House was converted into one large aviary with space to walk between the small mesh netting, which confined the birds, and the outer glass of the conservatory. As evidence of her love of birds, or so Cane thought, swans, a memento, he supposed, of the 'Swan Lake' ballet, swam in their slow stately way in the rather small pool in the lowest part of the gardens. The pool was surrounded by formal plantings backed on one side by a lawn and the drive was bordered by tall flowering shrubs. Just before she died Pavlova planted some 8,000 tulip bulbs in the borders.

Another commission for Cane was for a garden for the house which was to be presented by the Royal Warrant Holders' Association to King George V on his Jubilee in 1935. Designed by Beresford Marshall, the house, Georgian in character, stood on slightly high ground and gave extensive views of the wooded scenery of the Burhill golf-course in Surrey. Cane felt he was honoured to be asked to do the gardens for this house. But there were snags. For one thing he had to be particularly careful in his choice of materials because a number of firms were anxious to give materials and the gifts were both generous in quantity and varied. 'It was almost an "embarras de richesse": they not only gave more than was required but they tried in every way to give the quality that would fit best into the finished garden.'

It was necessary to provide an attractive setting and reasonable privacy without hiding any of the pleasant views across the golf-course. The garden had to be constructed more or less from scratch with nothing to consider other than some fully grown beeches, oaks, pines and birches, and the heather which grew profusely on the sandy soil. A paved forecourt with a large circular raised flower-pocket, the coping of the pocket high and wide enough to form a seat, was approached from the road by a curving drive. On the principal garden front the house opened up onto a terrace of York flagstone extending the length of the buildings and returning at right angles along its eastern façade. Across the lawn was made a paved rose-garden (also in genuine York stone) from which wide stone steps led down to a water-lily pool and a fountain figure in lead recessed into a yew hedge on the eastern boundary. A lawn bordered by curving beds framed a wide vista to the open spaces of the golf-course. In these beds mollis and Ghent azaleas were planted in large groups with hardy lilies growing among them while, to flower later, delphiniums from soft to deepest shades of blue and purple were used to increase the effect of distance. At its western end the lawn continued into a glade of rhododendrons and flowering shrubs and trees which, as well as providing a wealth of colour when they were in flower, made this part of the gardens completely private with banks of evergreen foliage. Groups of paeonies, hemerocallis, erigeron, phlox, lupins and other perennials planted among the flowering shrubs, with stretches of ericas which did well on this light soil, gave a succession of flowers. The flower pocket of the paved forecourt filled with scarlet geraniums provided a splash of brilliant colour against the warm tone of the brick façade and the setting of lawn and trees.

Although the house and garden were to have been a Jubilee gift to King George V, he died before it was ready and it was given to his successor King Edward VIII. Queen Mary went to Burhill to inspect the gift and was shown over the house by Beresford Marshall; she gave it a very thorough inspection. Then Cane had to show her round the gardens; he had to admit that, although the Queen quickly took in the general design, she was not as interested in the plants and their arrangements as she had been in the rooms and equipment of the house. She expressed approval of everything that had been done, however, and the company went into the drawing-room of the new house for tea. After tea the royal entourage left and Cane reflects that backs straightened and lighted cigarettes appeared almost before the royal cars had started on their way down the drive. A week later King Edward VIII went down to accept the gift formally. What a different atmosphere this time. Tea was served in the dining-room where smoking was allowed and conversation was loud and animated. The King appeared to Cane to be more interested in the gardens than Queen Mary had been and he showed by his questions a good knowledge of horticulture and plants in general.

Cane was at an international exhibition of the Royal Horticultural Society when Sir John Jarvis came by, remarking 'They have put you in an out-of-the-way corner, but I have found you at last,' a remark which was true, for Cane's exhibit was certainly not prominently placed. Sir John asked him to come to Hascombe Court, Godalming, and have a look at his gardens. He did so and made a complete tour with Sir John who, a man not given to wasting words, asked him to prepare a comprehensive plan for the treatment of the place as a whole. A few days later Cane presented Sir John with a preliminary design and was told to get the work started—this without waiting for the finished plans. The work was started almost immediately.

At Hascombe Court, the house with its entrance and one garden front built in local Bargate stone, the remainder in red brick and half timber, stood on a level plateau while from the terraces (designed by Sir Edwin Lutyens) and lawns the ground fell steeply to the south. This gave an uneasy impression that the house was perched on the edge of a precipice and might slide over.

It was an interesting though not an easy task. Scope existed for much variety of treatment. The herbaceous borders which extended for almost the length of the grounds from east to west were a feature. To Cane these borders showed no sense of colour harmony: strong pinks quarrelled with oranges and yellows, there was no gradation of colour, and the result was a discordant muddle. So the borders were emptied and replanted to a carefully prepared colour scheme. Sir John liked colour, strong colour, but one day he asked Cane if he thought that the colours in the middle length of the border were perhaps too strong. Cane replied that in his opinion they were not. The reasons for this were that they were in a green setting and that it was only in a particular fraction, less than one-third of the eastern borders, that they were really strong. Cane had designed the border so that softer colours at both ends worked up gradually to this strong centre grouping. In addition, the borders were seen against the green background of fruit and other trees, there was a wide lawn walk between them, and the flowers looked particularly well against the vivid green of the well-kept turf.

The gardens at Hascombe Court showed to a marked degree how necessary it is that the site should dictate the character of the design—one of Cane's basic principles in planning. With houses, rooms are usually rectangular or square and are comparatively easy to deal with. The details, such as cornices, skirtings, mouldings and panelling, are all to a considerable degree dictated by the general size and architectural character of the house. But with gardens this is not so. The garden designer has to take note of any existing feature on the site—trees, views, vistas, contours or levels, and water if present. Last, but certainly not least, come the wishes of the client. But Cane's attitude was that although these wishes must of course be given every consideration it was for the garden designer to interpret them and bring them into the scheme in the most effective way.

At Hascombe Court a straight drive passed through closely planted rhododendrons and turned at right angles into a spacious, severely plain, paved forecourt with the house facing, one wing projecting on the right. The entrance with a wide opening between its gate piers had no gates, the forecourt had its enclosing stone walls almost covered with the beautiful leaves of *Vitis Coignetiae,* clematis, and other climbing plants, and the glade was uncultivated ground.

Cane considered the drive narrow and without character so he had the rhododendrons removed and planted groups of Douglas Fir (*Abies Douglasii glauca*), *Juniperus chinensis* and other trees which, when they were grown to tall handsome specimens with plenty of mown turf between them and the drive on either side, made a far more dignified and useful approach to the spacious forecourt. At the entrance of the drive, wrought-iron gates were erected through which could be seen the trees and flowers of the gardens. The drive became a dignified composition of vertical and horizontal lines. The forecourt was left plain. On the southern side, reached through a door, the gardens were made to form a dramatic contrast to the plain forecourt. A wide terrace adjoined the house on its southern and western sides and to the west a lawn led between herbaceous borders to an extensive view of the near scenery. To the south a rock- and water-garden was built on the steeply sloping bank: the rock-garden, made with great blocks of stone, helped to support the southern terraces and the house itself on its southern elevation. There were a formal pool-garden, a long curving glade leading to the second, lower terrace at the southern boundary of the grounds and, connecting the lower terrace with the paved formal garden, a long curved walk bounded by trees and shrubs on one side, the other being left open to allow one to view the valley and rising hills in the distance.

Cane always liked to walk round these gardens whenever he visited Hascombe in later years. He would start from the forecourt and linger for a moment on the south terrace to enjoy the panorama of open sky, of turf sloping down to the village of Hascombe with its tiled roofs and church spire pointing to the sky. Then he would sometimes turn to the east and take the paved walk to the formal paved garden and through this pass the tennis-court and shelter, to enter the big glade with its fully grown cedar and other trees standing freely in an expanse of smooth turf. The glade swept on from here, its wide lawn enclosed on both sides by groups of flowering and foliage shrubs. Or at other times, descending several steps into the lower terrace over its stone boundary wall, he would enjoy another view of the village. The summer-house here was strategically positioned to enable the view to be enjoyed from it. At the eastern end of this terrace several steps brought him to the long walk which curved gently to yet another flight of steps and thence into the paved garden and back to the south terrace. From there he could make his way to the rock-garden on a steeply sloping bank and through a rhododendron wood—also on the steep slope—then up a staircase enclosed on both sides by walls of bamboos which, arching over to meet at the top, made a tunnel which always reminded Cane of the Scala d'Oro in Venice.

While Cane was making his gardens at Hascombe Court he was consulted by the Van den Berghs who had a house a few miles away: it was very large and they had decided to do away with part of it; they wanted advice on how to alter the garden to suit the smaller house.

On its main elevation the house opened out onto a wide lawn and because of the levels terracing was necessary. Cane decided on balustrading to enclose the lawn: it became a spacious terrace as well as one excellently suited to croquet. He designed gardens, formal and terraced, near the house. The upper terrace was adorned by two life-sized statues of gladiators facing each other across a level expanse of lawn—a fine example of how to place works of art successfully. When the house and gardens were finished, the Van den Berghs decided to hold a house-warming party and Cane was invited. Never one for such occasions he arrived early but he soon lost his shyness in the crowd of people who came to the party.

Around this time Cane was also asked to design a garden for the Armenian millionaire Nubar Gulbenkian's shooting-box near Aylesbury. He lunched with the Gulbenkians at their house and was very impressed by Gulbenkian who, despite his monocle and orchid, was a great personality and a very kind man. But though the plans were accepted the garden did not materialise.

Cane was called in to look at the gardens of Falkland Palace in

Fifeshire around 1947 and he at once saw that to design a setting for this historic palace would be an interesting challenge. Falkland is an ancient royal burgh with old houses and cobbled streets standing at the foot of the Lomond Hills. The Palace was the hunting palace of the Stuart dynasty and was always more of a home than a place of state. Here the Stuart kings and queens came to relax, spending their leisure in archery, tennis, falconry, and hunting stags through the glades and wild boar among the great oaks of the Forest of Falkland. In their quieter moments they banqueted, listened to music and poetry and played chess. The palace, despite its homeliness, is majestic in its architecture and the south range of the palace is the finest work of its period in Scotland. It has always remained the property of the Sovereign though no king or queen has resided there since Charles II ′and for centuries the palace has been left in the custody of hereditary keepers. Restoration work was carried out by the third Marquess of Bute who completely restored the south range and made it habitable again. He also undertook extensive research, tracing the foundations of the old well-house tower and consolidating what remains of the ruined east range. His work was continued by his son and grandson. In 1952 Major Michael Crichton-Stuart, the Hereditary Constable, Captain and Keeper of Falkland, appointed the National Trust for Scotland as Deputy Keeper of the Palace and handed the gardens over to them, making at the same time a generous endowment to ensure the future upkeep of the building and the grounds. Although a number of great gardens in Scotland have been and are being made over to the National Trust, the Falkland gardens are probably unique in that they were restored at considerable expense before being handed over to the Trust for the benefit of the public.

It was Cane's job to restore the gardens to the old royal plans. He found that from the palace windows one could see views extending beyond the courtyard to trees rising from turf and to gates on the eastern boundary; and he noted that the descending terraces were a succession of rather monotonous greens. He decided to design gardens which would retain the palace as it was but throw it into higher relief; he decided also to preserve and bring into the scheme what was left of the older palace, which

Opposite, top: Herbaceous border beneath the west wall at Falkland Palace, Fife
Opposite, bottom: Part of the new lower gardens at Falkland Palace

had been much larger. To accentuate the old walls which had been part of the original building he planted columnar-growing chamaecyparis at regular intervals on the higher levels so that these conifers, when they reached their full height, would make a pleasing composition of vertical and horizontal lines in addition to emphasising the plan of the former buildings. To provide colour, a formal long flower-border was made to run up to the space within the foundations of the old north range. To connect this border with the courtyard, steps were constructed to lead down to a flagged terrace along the lower garden wall. This terrace, enclosed on the north by low stone wall, led at its farther end to stone steps already in existence which in turn led down to the new lower gardens.

There were no existing flower-gardens at the palace but there had evidently been a garden below the ruins of the former banqueting hall in earlier times. This ground, entirely surrounded by walls, Cane made into a pleasure-garden with a central glade extending its entire length, containing walks between borders of paeonies, irises and lupins, following the lines of the enclosing walls. A long herbaceous border below the west wall was filled with flowers of soft colours and these contrasted with the stronger shades of those growing in borders on the south side. To save labour this border, which extended along the whole length of the garden, was planted up partly with flowering shrubs, but the transition from flowers to shrubs was gradual, groups of perennials being put among the shrubs and certain shrubs, chosen for their decorative foliage or because they flowered during the summer, among the herbaceous plants. Groups of cherry, weigela, ceanothus, philadelphus, cytisus and many other trees and shrubs gave height and substance to the area bordering the central glade. A formal rose-garden with a lily-pool and fountain at its centre made a contrast to the summer greens of the glade leading to it and the tennis-court built by King James V in 1539 (the only real-tennis court in Scotland to survive from the Stuart period) made an additional attraction.

Stonely Woods in Yorkshire, the home of Sir Charles Richmond Brown, was a long, low, narrow house with a broad forecourt on the northern side and a wide terrace on the southern. From the forecourt the ground rose steeply to the north with the result that the forecourt was

Opposite: The rotunda and part of the terrace gardens at Stonely Woods, Yorkshire

sheltered. The paved terrace served as the main pleasure-garden and was divided into three, a rose-garden and two gardens of roses, shrubs and flowering plants. An open-fronted loggia at the western end looked out onto a rose-garden. In the loggia a fireplace large enough to burn logs enabled one to sit in chilly Yorkshire weather within sight and scent of the roses and enjoy them in comfort. A broad flagged walk went from the garden door through the middle one of the three gardens into which the terrace was divided to a semicircular seat built out into the meadow beneath. Cane liked to stand at the end of the terrace and look out to the mass of flowers and foliage which in its variety of colour reminded him a little of the large marquee at the Chelsea Flower Show in its early stages before it had been tidied up and order had emerged.

Lady Richmond Brown introduced Cane to Lord Feversham who lived at Nawton Tower not far from Stonely Woods. At Nawton Tower the principal reception-rooms, the drawing-room, study and dining-room all opened out onto a terrace. At dinner one evening the treatment of this terrace was discussed. It was the connecting link between the house and the garden and Lord Feversham thought it ought to be balustraded. But Cane said instantly, 'I don't think I would have it balustraded but I would have continuous steps unbroken from end to end of the terrace.' Lord Feversham said, 'I believe you've got it.' The steps were built and some handsome pots were bought to stand in suitable places and in a straight row on the terrace. Everyone was pleased, including Cane. There were five steps in all and their unbroken length gave an air of dignity to the scene, yet in the simplest way. Lord Feversham had done extensive alterations to his gardens before Cane was called in but he was always sympathetic to any suggestions. From the lawn to which the terrace steps went down a wide walk of grass continued to a glade in the lower part of the garden. Cane altered the curving lines of the border to fit in with an overall curve to which everything in the glade was to conform. It brought into the general scheme a Scots pine that was particularly fine in its shape and the glade as a whole became a fitting termination to the intervening set of gardens.

Another scheme introduced by Cane at Nawton Tower was to wall in the forecourt and enclose both ends of the terrace with walls. This gave more shelter—something that is very necessary in the Yorkshire climate.

From the village of Oakley in Bedfordshire one turns into a straight

The informal water-garden, once a tennis-court, at Westfields, Bedfordshire

drive over a mile long at the end of which is Westfields, which belonged to Eric Davison. When Cane saw it first it stood in the centre of its own woodlands and park. There were lawns on which limes and other trees gave a feeling of age, and a tennis-court enclosed with low brick walls. Cane's opinion was that the grounds were neither extensive enough nor interesting enough to be in keeping with the size and character of the house. It was monotonous, with few highlights or unexpected changes of scenery. But he saw opportunities and asked for more land on the north on which he made additional lawns and glades. A rose-garden was constructed at the end of the lawn onto which the house opened and the tennis-court was changed into an informal water-garden. Part of a wall which separated the gardens from the surrounding land was removed and this allowed the wide turf

borders of the drive to sweep unbroken into the first lawn onto which the house opened in its main garden elevation. The rose-garden was paved with its entrance marked by two carved stone baskets of fruit, on stone pedestals. For some time, however, Mrs. Davison did not like the rose-garden: to her it did not look quite finished. On one of Cane's visits he was asked if it now looked better. Without at first quite seeing what the difference was, Cane replied, 'Yes, it does.' The Davisons had planted a short length of yew hedge on each side from the wall to the pedestal, leaving the semicircle of turf framed as it were on both sides. The rose-garden was enclosed and yet open, for the curve of the turf carried one's eye right into the roses.

When the decision to change the tennis-court into a water-garden was made the Davisons could not make up their minds whether they wanted it formal or informal. Cane too was undecided for once, and prepared two designs, one formal and the other informal. He showed them to the Davisons and the decision—unanimous—was in favour of the informal one. So a long curving stream, confined within its banks by large blocks of water-worn Westmorland stone, was made to fall steeply from the highest point; it was possible, in fact necessary, to make several pools from the highest point to the lowest and largest pool which was constructed within sight of the principal living-room windows. The new watercourse looked so natural after a while that it might always have been there. A more formal water-garden was made in what had been the forecourt and this, together with the informal water-garden, the rose-garden and an herbaceous border flanking the long lawn nearest the house, all of which were bounded by a long straight walk to the east which merged at the eastern end into an extension of the central glade, made a comprehensive set of gardens in which every part of the total area was used to the greatest advantage.

One of the things Cane liked best about his life was that it brought him into contact with a large number of delightful people, many of whom became his intimate friends. One such friendship was formed with Mr. and Mrs. Egbert Barnes at whose house, Hungerdown at Seagry near Chippenham in Wiltshire, he enjoyed many delightful visits. The first time

Opposite, top: Rose-garden and pool at Westfields
Opposite, bottom: Steps to the lily-pool from the terrace at Hungerdown House

View of the glade from the upper terrace at Hungerdown House

Lily-pools and steps surmounted by a magnificent oak at Hungerdown House, Wiltshire

he went to Hungerdown he found that where there should have been a luxuriance of flowering trees and plants, there were neat rows of cabbages, carrots and onions which, thought Cane, 'nice as they are on the dinner table . . . are not really satisfying to gaze on from the principal sitting-rooms!'

The house on a site occupying a sloping shelf overlooking the upper Avon Valley had wide views to east and south over broad pastures. The architectural character of the house demanded a certain amount of formality in its immediate surroundings and, to give a sense of stability as well, plenty of terracing, steps and retaining walls were necessary. So to give formality to the immediate surroundings the terraced area was extended and the long front lawn taken round the south side of the house. From the terrace a flight of steps was made to lead down from its southern end into a pool-garden which became the focal turning-point from the long terrace into the gardens, still formal, which led through a sundial-garden into the informal formality of a cherry walk. The pool-garden, paved with radiating stones and having at its centre a circular pool with a lead figure spouting water into a stone basin, was a focal point between the south and east terraces. On the right of the pool-garden, steps rose to a lawn dominated by a large oak which cast its spreading shadow over the grass. Another flight of steps led up to the formal sundial-garden. It was this garden at Hungerdown which led A. G. L. Hellyer, a man with a great knowledge of garden design, to write (in *Country Life*):

> Hungerdown House . . . displays nearly all the principles that he (Percy Cane) regards as of greatest importance in garden design. These may be summarised as a firm base for the house to stand on and agreeable contrast between the various parts of the garden. There are to be terraces and paved areas leading to woodland glades; areas of dense planting contrasted with open spaces, where grass and clipped shrubs provide the principal decoration; fine trees and shrubs contrasted with herbaceous plants and water used for the light that it brings into a garden, for its reflections and the many moisture-loving plants that can be grown in and around it.

At another time Cane went to Aughentaine at Fivemiletown in Northern Ireland, the home of Captain Hamilton-Stubber. He had already looked at the photographs of the house and had been told that the Captain and his

Lawn dominated by oak tree at Hungerdown House

wife were undecided whether or not to have the house demolished and a new one built on the same site. To Cane the house, which was an old Irish castle, seemed to have so much character as to warrant its retention. But he was told that however picturesque it might look from outside the proportions of its rooms were bad and it was difficult to run. So the old castle was demolished and a new house, long and proportionally rather low, erected on the site of the old building. From the entrance gates a long drive passed through woods—partly newly planted, partly consisting of established trees—which skirted a lake, with trees going down to the water's edge. Reaching the forecourt it was necessary to go round or through the house to reach the terrace which was wide and long and overlooked gardens of a type Cane felt the biblical hanging gardens of Babylon might have been. From the terrace a stairway took the easiest way

New house and forecourt planning at Aughentaine, N. Ireland

Paved garden at Aughentaine

to the bottom of the steep bank which was planted with bold groups of low-growing shrubs.

One evening, while the new house at Aughentaine was being built, Cane was quietly reading in the lounge of the local hotel when a man came in by the front entrance, passed behind him and, taking hold of the book he was reading, threw it into a corner. He then went out by a back door as suddenly as he had come. No one seemed to know who the man was and all Cane could do was to retrieve his book and ponder a little on the strange habits of the Irish!

The first time Cane went to Lord Lothian's home at Monteviot, near Jedburgh, he had written to say he would arrive at Berwick by train at around half-past six in the morning but he was relieved when Lord Lothian replied suggesting that he came at a less ungodly hour. At Monteviot the house stood on a plateau overlooking the River Teviot flowing in the valley below. The drive swept into the forecourt through a short but beautiful piece of scenery and there in front was the main elevation of the house, the tall narrow windows of the great hall carried through two storeys. To the right, low walls separated the forecourt from the gardens while to the left a range of buildings completed the feeling of enclosure. It was all spacious, Scottish, and sheltered—this last a welcome attribute in the Scottish climate. On the main garden front the design had to be subservient to the lovely view of the river. The length and formality of the terrace which extended from end to end of the gardens was made even more apparent by a flagged stone path, which continued along the whole length of the terrace and seemed to unify the varying elevations of the pile of buildings.

To keep the view of the river unbroken, the central length of the sloping turf bank, which was too steep to walk down and which gave an uncomfortable feeling that the upper terrace was not adequately supported, was changed by Cane into three terraces to give two more or less even slopes with a level turf walk between them. By this simple device the highest parts of the banks were kept below eye level and the view was not interrupted. Flower-gardens were made at the western end of the upper terrace and following a path with a breast-high wall to protect people from falling into the lower gardens came a terraced rose-garden paved with York stone with behind it the wall rising to the higher platform on which Monteviot House stood. The rose-garden was enclosed at one end by a

The River Teviot seen from a wall shelter at Monteviot, Scotland

Part of the river garden at Monteviot

stone wall and at the opposite or western end by walls and thick, high yew
hedges. To the north, a lower retaining wall was built to sitting height to
offer a convenient and continuous seat from which to enjoy the prospect of
the park-like meadows falling gradually to the river. Another garden east of
the rose-garden sloped gently to a landing-stage. On each side of the
river-garden were parallel wide borders filled with shrub and floribunda
roses, and with large groups of delphiniums and other herbaceous plants
between these. Behind these borders were turf walks again backed by yet
other wide borders filled with shrubs.

It was while he was at Monteviot that Cane met a Mrs. Carr whose
home was Ditchingham Hall, near Bungay in Suffolk. When he was invited
to Ditchingham, the car took him through handsome wrought-iron gates

The approach to the house at Drum-na-Vullin, Scotland

into a drive that swept through a well-timbered park to the principal entrance. To the west of the forecourt, with a background of prunus and other trees, a long, wide herbaceous border gave a splendid mass of colour. Although not conforming with usual practice, this border seemed both right in its position and in its bold groupings of colour. To give more colour a rose-garden had been made below the terrace. But one of the grandest features, Cane felt, was a cedar walk—in fact, cedars seemed to him to be the glory of Ditchingham Hall.

Another Scottish visit was to Miss Sylvia Campbell's place at Drum-na-Vullin, near Lochgilphead in Argyllshire. He went by train to Glasgow and on by steamer to Lochgilphead through some of the loveliest of countryside. At Drum-na-Vullin the principal windows looked out onto typical west-coast scenery, and outside the front door there was a low wall to prevent one from falling down the slope and into the river below. Following Miss Campbell around some recently acquired land on the far side of the stream, Cane kept finding that from time to time she would disappear into a hollow, such was the unevenness of the ground. But he considered the grounds unique in their combination of gardens and scenery. He made various alterations and when it was all over a letter came to him from Miss Campbell which said simply, 'Thanks to you I think the garden at "Drum" will be the garden of my dreams and I am grateful.' Which is about the nicest thing that can be said to a garden architect.

It was a red-letter day for Cane when Mr. and Mrs. Leonard Elmhirst came to consult him about the treatment of the grounds at Dartington Hall, near Totnes in Devon. He had, of course, heard of Dartington: the very name sounded musical and he had always wanted to go there. He arrived on a perfect June evening and was able to see Dartington Hall in all its glory, standing in the midst of some of Devon's loveliest scenery. The long drive was bordered with richly wooded pasture-land, rising on the one side and sloping on the other through grey lichen-covered oaks and beeches down to the silvery River Dart. The Hall, its grey stone walls softly lit by the rays of the setting sun and its lawns chequered by the shadows of large trees, looked so lovely that he wondered if there was anything that he would be able to suggest that would be an improvement.

Next morning he explored the grounds and realised that, lovely and unusual as the setting for the Hall was, its possibilities had not been fully

The azalea dell at Dartington Hall, Devon

*Opposite: The stairway connecting the upper glade
with the lower lawn at Dartington*

appreciated. The terraces which the principal gardens overlooked descended in a series of levels to the bottom of an open-air theatre to rise on the far side in giant steps of turf. The formality of their banks and levels, so right in turf, would have been wrong in masonry but the dramatic feeling of height and depth was increased still further by the wall of the Hall rising from the south terrace and by the magnificent chestnut trees that crowned the highest level of the open-air theatre. These terraces had been constructed in the fourteenth century by the builder of the Hall, John Holland, Duke of Exeter. They were the work of a master planner and Cane realised at once that they should not be altered. The walks to the north of the open-air theatre, too, were made just where they fitted most easily into the rising slopes.

One thing, however, became fairly obvious as he made his way round: one condition—a condition almost essential in larger gardens—was lacking: there was no clear way in which one could make a tour of the grounds and also, whilst the position for the Hall and its existing gardens had been so well chosen, the visual relation of vistas to the scenery beyond the confines of the gardens left much to be desired. And again, although the grounds had a large and varied collection of trees, shrubs and plants some of it was too mixed. There was a lack of character in some of the gardens and walks.

Cane was not, of course, the first landscape designer to be called in to help with Dartington Hall. In 1927 H. Avray Tipping, the editor of *Country Life*, had planned part of the garden close to the house, using yew hedges to enclose the private lawn and the bowling-green, manoeuvring the difficult angles in such a way that the result successfully concealed the problem. Then Stewart Lynch took charge of the gardens for many years and was responsible for a number of valuable shrubs and the successful attempt to clear the space that became an open-air theatre. In 1933 Beatrix Farrand, an American garden designer, brought order to the courtyard and designed a cobbled drive to encircle the central lawn. She levelled the ground in front of the private house making a small terrace and a path running alongside the old kitchen, and to open out the garden she created paths and connecting links.

Cane, who had been suggested to the Elmhirsts by Constance Spry, went there first in 1945 and he at once saw the possibilities of cutting

The spacious glade and vista to the rising hills at Dartington

through the thick, wild overgrown upper areas in order to open up vistas and to create special features of interest. The glade and the long flight of steps below leading down to the lower end of the tournament ground are part of his creation. The site of the glade had been a tangle of more or less wild undergrowth but after Cane had had the ground cleared, the borders dug and planted, the lawn sown and a spacious glade of flowering trees and shrubs with evergreen backgrounds of conifers and hollies constructed, it was possible to look over the lower gardens and onto the rising hills in the distance. Cane felt that this view, always superb, rising group behind group and with misty shadows shot in certain lights with silvery pink, violet, or purple, had all the loveliness of a Chinese landscape painted on silk.

At the lower end of the glade he made his long stairway on what was a bank clothed with ericas with narrow paths winding through it, an untidy interlude in the midst of what had become a principal vista. The upper glade needed adequate connection with the lower lawn so the stairway was constructed to give this. Seen from below with the straight trunks of tall trees rising from the ground at the top and seeming to carry height upwards, or from above, with extensive views over richly wooded country, it gave the necessary connecting link, uniting and making one conception of the upper glade, the stairway and the lower lawn. Proportionately wide, and with landings to make the ascent easy, the stairway was an essential part of one of the longest vistas. He cleared High Meadow and made it a pleasant upper region of the garden with a fresh vista to the Hall. Other parts of the garden too, under his direction, were cleared and simplified: a new entrance drive was constructed, the upper road remade and the azalea dell created.

Cane always felt that of the many gardens he had designed that at Dartington Hall was one of the most interesting to do owing to its nature, its romantic surroundings and, especially, the consideration he invariably received for any suggestions he put forward. Mrs. Elmhirst had the most critical eye for form he had ever come across. When he paid a visit to Dartington he usually arrived in the evening and discussed general plans over dinner. Then next morning he and J. Johnson (head gardener until he died in 1962, when he was succeeded by T. L. Underhill) would tour the gardens or those parts of it in which the Elmhirsts were particularly interested. Johnson was a pleasant, capable man who managed his staff with considerable tact with the result that the garden department ran very smoothly. It was Johnson who devised the scheme of collaboration with Devon County Council to train boys for future work in gardens, public parks and nurseries and also introduced weekend courses for enthusiastic amateur gardeners. Johnson was more interested in the horticultural side of his work than in the general design of the gardens. Cane, on the other hand, though interested in the plants and the horticultural side of the gardens to a certain extent, was primarily concerned with the overall treatment of the gardens. He was in the habit, before joining the head gardener on the official tour, of having a walk round on his own first so that he could consider the design of the grounds quietly in its wider aspects. At one time he was asked to look at the small rock-garden which, made on a slight hill, had a paved walk going through it. Johnson told him that he could not see anything wrong with it and, what was more, neither could any of the many parks superintendents, head gardeners and other qualified gardeners who had visited Dartington. But Cane had other ideas. 'All right', he said to Johnson, 'lend me a couple of your men and you sit there and watch what I do'. He then proceeded to correct a few of what he considered mistakes such as the balance of the very large boulders of which the rock-garden was constructed. It received Mrs. Elmhirst's favourable comment but Johnson said nothing.

Dartington under Cane and the other designers became a garden where form dominated design and the contours of the land were used to intensify the natural effects of height and depth and distance. The trees and shrubs were used to give structure to the composition, and the lawns to emphasize space. The extensive use of evergreens helped to provide interest throughout the winter. The great trees, planted by the Champernowne family, stood in grandeur, and vistas gave great sweeps to distance views and linked the gardens with the surrounding countryside.

The Dutch people in 1946 decided that they would like to give a memorial garden to England as a mark of their appreciative recognition of the hospitality accorded to their Queen and government during the German occupation of their country. The donors suggested that this garden should be at Coventry as in its suffering from German bombing the city had had an experience similar to that of Rotterdam. Cane was asked to design it. The Dutch government sent over a very fine collection of plants and left it to Cane to make the best use of them. The main garden—there were three—was made on an open space in the centre of the city and it had to fit in with the civic planning scheme. The meant that it had to be formal and that the shrubs and plants should not be so tall as to separate it noticeably from the surrounding thoroughfare. It had also to form a setting for Sir William Dick's statue of Lady Godiva in the centre of the square. Cane designed a garden having wide, shallow steps at each side and at the cathedral end, the statue rising from the level lawn at the central focal point formed by the vistas down the length of and across the garden.

Although the statue was not completed in time the garden was opened on the arranged date by Princess Elizabeth, as she then was. On the day of the ceremony, Cane made a special journey to Coventry to make sure everything was all right. Imagine his horror when he found that every

Part of the memorial garden given by the Dutch people to the City of Coventry

empty space between the masses of chiefly pink rhododendrons had been thickly planted with bright orange marigolds. 'I had nothing against marigolds: among harmonious colours they look well; but with the pink rhododendrons, equally strong in their own rich masses of colour, the result was ghastly'. Something had to be done, and quickly! Cane spoke to the person in charge and was told that 'Nature never makes mistakes' to which Cane replied that this clashing of colours was not Nature's doing. He managed to get the marigolds replaced with heathers; the result, if not so striking, was at least harmonious. Then when the procession started to make its stately progress through the gardens Cane found that the official robes worn by the mayor and corporation were of a rusty red colour almost as discordant with the pink rhododendrons as the orange marigolds. He returned to London defeated.

Another occasion on which things went wrong was at St. Anne's Hill, Chertsey, to which Cane gave some formal architectural treatment as a contrast to the mature trees with which the park was already well furnished. He designed two temples and a terrace balustrade but had to make do with just the terrace balustrade which was placed in the centre of the park where there was a sudden drop from a higher level to the valley. The terrace was extended for a considerable distance and instead of a temple at either end Cane put a seat which completed the treatment quite satisfactorily.

Cane made no attempt at St. Anne's Hill to create a public park. It was to be a beauty spot and nothing as banal even as beds of geraniums might be allowed within its confines. Instead one was to wander through stretches of natural woodland with here and there generously wide seats that would provide accommodation for quite a number of people in carefully chosen places which gave extensive views over the Thames Valley with the river shining in the distance. St. Anne's Hill was a lovely stretch of scenery within easy motoring distance of London and had become popular with visitors from that city and miles around. Cane always found the love of city dwellers for real country interesting. Once as a child, on being taken to London to stay with friends, he had remarked of one of the London parks, 'But this is artificial; it is not real country'. Since then, however, he had learnt to value the parks of London and other cities at their true worth for even if they were rather sophisticated they were like lungs through which the earth could fulfil its necessary task of breathing, a function otherwise impossible in the cities and towns with their surfaces sealed by acres of buildings and hard surfaced roads.

Lady Berry had consented to open the park officially and a gold key had been specially cut for the occasion. Everything was arranged and all should have been well. But when Cane went round early to make sure that nothing was wrong he found that a lorry had bumped into the gates with the consequence that the gold key would not work. The damage could not be repaired in time for the opening ceremony so Cane on arriving for the official luncheon at Sir Gomer Berry's house explained to Lady Berry what had happened. When it came to the opening the gate was left unlocked. Lady Berry tactfully pretended to use the gold key and no one was any the wiser.

Something rather different for Cane was the designing of a setting for the offices and laboratories of the Anglo-Iranian Oil Company on the Isle

A garden in progress for the Anglo-Iranian Oil Company at Isle of Grain, Kent

of Grain in the Thames Estuary. He visited the site on a cold windy autumn day and realised that it would be an interesting but difficult task—difficult mainly because of the cold, wind-swept site, which meant that only very hardy shrubs could be used. And apart from climate and exposure there were certain other limitations with regard to the trees and shrubs which could be employed: for example, because of its inflammable nature the common gorse, *Ulex europaeus,* was out of the question. Again, certain deciduous trees and shrubs had to be avoided because of risk of injury to the oil pipes.

Another place where care had to be taken in the choice of shrubs was at the Middlesex Hospital Convalescent Home at Clacton in Essex where, despite the presence of a shelter belt, the salt-laden winds still made it necessary to use reasonably hardy subjects. And because the cost of maintaining the home had to be met out of private funds, ease and economy of upkeep were of particular importance. But with the help of seats and shelters, spacious lawns, long straight borders in front of the building and an extensive glade leading to an enclosed formal garden, the

A garden glade at Chestham Park, Sussex

grounds eventually fulfilled their purpose and provided a scene of peace and seclusion in a setting rich with the colours and fragrance of flowers and foliage.

Prince Littler's comfortable modern house was at Chestham Park, near Henfield in Sussex. From the road an avenue of limes went through the park to the principal entrance: there was no separate forecourt, the house opening directly onto the extensive gardens which included fine old forest trees, rhododendrons and azaleas and a number of smaller flowering trees and shrubs, a hard tennis-court, large lawns and rose-beds—in fact all the ingredients for lovely, interesting gardens. But unfortunately no cohesive plan had been followed and the gardens thus lacked form and balance.

In very large gardens, a separate forecourt has definite advantages and at Chestham Park a second door opened onto ground which Cane saw could easily be made into a forecourt with generous parking space. The door, approached by an arched covered way something like a short cloister, would, he felt, be suitable for the principal entrance. A cupressus hedge,

A lily-pool in beautiful surroundings at Chestham Park

thick and tall enough to ensure privacy, was planted to separate the drive from the gardens, to which a wrought-iron gate gave access. A few necessary alterations were made to the new forecourt and the improvement, both in convenience and appearance, was entirely satisfactory. Now there were both space and pleasant vistas onto the park—everything, in fact, needed in the creation of lovely gardens. To the south the house opened onto a spreading lawn. There a wide paved terrace was laid, a connecting link between the house and the lawn, the latter being bounded by groups of tall old rhododendrons interplanted with perpetual flowering shrub roses and hardy liliums, *L. auratum* and the tall *L. tigrinum splendens*.

On the eastern elevation a large sun-room was a pleasant and useful feature. Centring on this a turf walk was cut through existing trees and shrubs to the boundary on this side. The back of a specially made thirty-foot-wide stone seat enhanced by its level lines the effect of the rounding masses of trees in the park beyond. Near the house the borders were filled with herbaceous plants in a carefully designed colour scheme. To have made the whole length herbaceous would have been monotonous and would have meant too much maintenance. About halfway down the walk a mature oak spread its gnarled branches over the turf and from here the remainder of the walk was planted thickly with azaleas and lilies. It was an unexpected and agreeable change; the azaleas flowered earlier than the herbaceous plants and later were resplendent with the crimsons and golds of their autumn foliage. Using the gnarled oak tree halfway down the walk as a turning point Cane cut another grass walk to lead into a new rose-garden enclosed by yew hedges and with each bed planted with just one variety of rose. It was the principal formal garden.

Cane always liked to have water in his larger gardens but at Chestham Park no water, not even a fountain, was to be seen. He managed to get some from a spring, bringing it over gently sloping ground which lent itself to the making of several waterfalls. A water course, bounded by boulders of lovely water-worn Westmorland stone was made, goldfish were introduced into the pools, and everyone was pleased—except the goldfish, which were soon eaten by herons.

One weekend Cane was invited to Cliveden, Lord Astor's estate near Taplow in Buckinghamshire. He arrived for lunch on the Saturday and sat next to Mr., afterwards Sir, John Maude. Lady Astor was splendid as a hostess and was both animated and interesting, able to draw the best of talk and information from her guests. Cane found it an intellectual treat just to sit and listen to the lively remarks and repartee that went on across the table. Conversation ranged over many subjects: politics, travel, art, and a whole range of other interests, were discussed at some length. The different views held by the guests threw many new sidelights on current affairs and, although Cane was a little vague in his thoughts, he certainly went home on the Sunday with many ideas to think over. One example of Lady Astor's consideration for her guests was that she arranged for a night-porter to be on duty to serve them. The gardens of course interested Cane. From the high terrace a wonderful view was made even finer by what appeared to be a mist of blue stretching from below the terrace almost to the river. The blue mist effect was achieved by a parterre of box-edged beds below the terrace where, instead of each bed being filled with plants of different

colours, every one was planted with *Nepeta mussinii*. In full flower the effect was charming and, moreover, the blue did, as blue so often does, make the garden seem longer. Cane found it a pleasure just to wander about the grounds.

Lady Dugan, whose husband was Governor of the State of Victoria in Australia, had a house at Deddington in Oxfordshire. Cane visited it several times. The house was an almost perfect example of Elizabethan architecture on a comparatively small scale. Built on a high boundary wall, the church, of much the same period as the Castle House, dominated and immensely enhanced the forecourt. The Castle House contained a priest's hole. The gardens, enclosed by old stone walls, were an attractive combination of the formal and the informal. About halfway down the length of the lawn, a difference in levels—which gave the opportunity for steps to extend the width of the garden—added a lot of interest and, because the lawn sloped down from the house gave, too, the feeling of a greater distance than actually existed.

An unusual assignment for Cane and one which taxed his skill was to design the gardens for a model village. This was at the Avoncroft Museum of Buildings, Stoke Prior, Bromsgrove, Worcestershire, a museum inaugurated by L. G. Harris, whose aim it was to collect from a wide radius various buildings connected with industries and to rebuild them in as attractive and suitably related a setting as possible.

Opposite: An 'almost perfect' example of Elizabethan architecture at Castle House, Deddington, Oxfordshire

4
International Designer

While Cane was designing a garden for Captain Tudor-Crosthwaite at Little Bowden, Pangbourne, in Berkshire, in the early 1920s, Mrs. Tudor-Crosthwaite told him that she thought her father, Mr. Stoneham, would like to see him at Le Touquet. Cane was delighted to have the chance of a professional job on the Continent. Up to that time, except for an occasional trip to the French Riviera for pleasure, he had not been abroad. He quickly made the necessary arrangements and went.

Stoneham was a well-known person in Le Touquet. He was more or less the instigator of Le Touquet as a pleasure resort and it was he who was said to have persuaded the railway authorities to get some of the Paris Rapides to stop at Etaples, the station for Le Touquet. Cane often stood on the low platforms at Etaples and watched the Rapides go thundering through seeming to him extremely powerful just because he was so near and saw so much of their wheels. The golf-course at Le Touquet is one of the finest in the world and popular with English people because of its being within easy reach of London, Dover, and Folkestone. Stoneham and a friend arranged for Cane to have an exhibition at the golf club-house of designs, sketches, and photographs of gardens he had designed—a gesture which Cane much appreciated and which led to several commissions around Le Touquet. His knowledge of French now came in handy.

Arthur Kemp, whom Cane first met at Le Touquet, was to Cane an example of the finest type of American. Born into wealth and leisure he lived wisely. He loved England, and Cane, knowing this, asked him one day why he did not buy a small property in Britain. His answer was 'I know that I collect various things, but I do not collect houses'. At that time the Kemps already had a house in Paris, another in Le Touquet and a flat in Monte Carlo. Mme Kemp was an inveterate gambler and Cane escorted her one evening to the casino at Le Touquet where she proceeded to 'break the bank'. Cane was no gambler himself but he realised that 'breaking the bank' meant considerable financial gain to Mme Kemp. Arthur Kemp, too, was no gambler and when Cane was staying at their house the two of them often spent the evening talking, reading or just being lazy and doing nothing. The Kemps dined late so there was not much time after dinner. As regards the Kemps' gardens at Le Bungalow, which were the reason for Cane being there, Mme Kemp usually appeared about midday and took Cane on a tour of them.

The garden that Cane finally created for the Kemps was slightly Japanese in design and he took a lot of trouble to give it that perfection of balance and arrangement in the various plants, shrubs and other materials that is typical of good Japanese work. The garden seemed to merge imperceptibly into the surrounding forest of pines and silver birches. There were also a rose-garden partly enclosed by a brick pergola, and a herbaceous border.

Sad to relate, practically every tree in this garden was destroyed in World War II, and the house was damaged. A cottage in the grounds, however, was restored and gardens made on a site part of which had been kitchen-garden, the remainder rough grass under pines and birches, the trees of the district. The soil at Le Touquet is almost pure sand, sand which is gradually becoming fertile. The entrance to The Cottage as it was named was by a private drive from which a short flagged path was laid to the door. There could be nothing elaborate: the keynote of the gardens had to be simplicity, a simplicity derived from good proportions and lovely colours, but the gardens could be given distinction. On the entrance front, panels of turf were laid on each side of the flagged path with, at each end of the turf panels, a bed of scarlet geraniums. Tubs on either side of the door were filled, too, with geraniums which, with several old silver birches in the lawn, made a pleasing scene of silver and scarlet in their green setting. Fortunately only in the pleasure-grounds had the trees been destroyed. Around the cottage, a delightful one-storey building, were birches and pines, their trunks silvery and gnarled with age. Flagstones were brought from Yorkshire and used for a paved terrace which, enclosed by dwarf walls built at either end, was laid for the length of the cottage on its garden front. From the terrace two continuous flights of steps led down to a lawn which extended to a background of trees and shrubs on the eastern boundary. The borders on both sides of the lawn were filled with flowers—delphiniums, Monarda Cambridge Scarlet, white Shasta daisies, erigeron, phlox, Michaelmas daisies, *Nepeta mussinii* and other perennials. And between them, plenty of annual flowers in large groups. Lavender and rosemary, ten-week stocks, heliotrope and mignonette added fragrance to the colour of the garden. On each side of the lawn, paving was laid to increase the formality of the garden which at its far end had a fountain figure in lead spouting water into a circular basin, set in flagstones and forming, with the seat behind it, an attractive and distinctive feature. Roses grow well at Le Touquet, so a paved rose-garden was made with, as its central feature, an Italian well-head in Istrian marble. Seen down the length of the lawn the rose-garden was a parterre in rich colour. To the west of the centre garden the lawn was continued into a glade in which were left several groups of silver birches. Around the lawn lilacs, cherries, laburnums, magnolias and other shrubs, with yet more groups of annuals, made a garden in which the borders, following the lines of the boundaries, were gay with flowers. The final effect, with the birches and pines, the long wide formal flower-walk, the rose-garden and its spreading lawns, was to make the gardens at The Cottage merging into their setting of trees a most pleasant summer retreat.

Cane was to make many visits to France both professionally and for pleasure. In Les Hauts de Saint Paul behind Nice he designed a garden at La Bergerie for M. Poupon. The house was Provençal and had plenty of character, with a view of the Mediterranean spreading into the distance and merging with the sky and colour of the grey-green pines and the even greyer olives which clothed the intervening hills to give a study in pastel shading. In front of the house the wide terrace extended to a pavilion which was often used as a dining-room and from this terrace a lawn path banked with flowers was constructed which led directly to a swimming-pool at the sunny end of which was an open-fronted shelter. This being the Mediterranean the swimming-pool was, of course, the social rendezvous of the gardens. Except for paving outside the pavilion it was surrounded by turf. Turf in the warm southern climate is particularly pleasant to walk on. A glade with borders of flowering shrubs was made beyond the swimming-pool and the drive.

While staying at Cannes with friends, Cane met Lady Yule, the widow of Sir David Yule who was said to have left her something in the region of

£12 million. Cane was invited to her yacht the *Nahlin,* at that time lying at anchor in Cannes harbour. He was shown over it and though he had always been a bad sailor the thought of yachting in such luxurious conditions almost made him enjoy the thought, at any rate, of going to sea. But pressing engagements brought him back to London and work. Eventually he did design a small garden for Lady Yule at Cagnes, a village between Cannes and Nice. By using large trees in tubs, which are sold by most of the Riviera nurseries, he was able to produce for her a garden completely furnished from the time of planting. The house was Provençai in its architecture and he found making the garden a very interesting task. The other garden he did for her was in England, at Bricket Wood in Hertfordshire. This had terraces, an informal water-garden with a bridge, and lawns with borders of shrubs and flowering plants. Lunching one day with Lady Yule's secretary, Cane remarked how nice it must be not to have to consult one's bank-book before buying anything one wanted. The secretary replied that Lady Yule might not be as fortunate as Cane thought. She had to be constantly on her guard against overcharging and she asked Cane to be sure to get alternative prices for anything he was having done, without giving Lady Yule's name.

Arthur Kemp, whom we have met previously, was one of the governors of the American Hospital of Paris at Neuilly-sur-Seine and he invited Cane to the hospital to suggest a treatment for the grounds. Pleasantly situated with a number of mature trees to relate it to the well-treed surroundings, it stood in a pleasant suburb of Paris. Cane realised it needed a rather special treatment, not quite as a garden yet as something more than a park. In any case the grounds were not extensive enough for a park, at least for one in the British sense of the word. Tennis-courts were provided for the staff and for those patients who were well enough to play. One condition, however, had to be complied with. There must be a dry walk running right round the site, chiefly for the benefit of those patients who, not being well enough to walk, had to be wheeled round in bath chairs. It was also essential that there should not be trees near to the windows to block light and air. The site was level and reasonably open, and consisted mainly of rectangular spaces of lawn which could be seen from most of the hospital windows. The gardens, before they were altered, had little distinction and it was necessary for Cane to prepare a scheme which would give them character, interest

Trees planted well away from the building in order not to block the view at the American Hospital, Paris

and especially plenty of colour for as long a part of the year as possible. The straight lines of the boundary walls called for straight walks and borders and rectangular lawns similar to those often seen in the walled gardens of Georgian houses in Great Britain. But character could be given by more interesting planting; the colour could be more varied, harmonious and very much richer; and by using flagstones for the walks the gardens would appear larger and finer than with gravel paths. From a raised terrace onto which the central hall of the hospital opened there was a long view of the grounds. From the terrace a flight of steps was constructed which descended to a flagged path wide enough to accommodate invalid chairs and following the lines of the boundaries so that it was possible to make a complete circuit of the gardens on paving. Borders round the western lawn were planted with roses against a background of lilac, philadelphus and other flowering shrubs. The shrubs, which became banks of colour in the spring, were followed by the flowers of the roses. Behind the bedding roses

Cane put *Rosa moyesii, Rosa hugonis, Rosa willmottiae* and other species which looked lovely with their graceful, arching, flower-laden stems.

A roomy, semi-octagonal seat with a sundial standing by it provided an attractive feature opposite the terrace and stairway from the principal garden entrance to the hospital. Borders on each side of the seat were filled with tulips for spring colour followed by bedding dahlias for summer and autumn, the varieties being chosen so that their colours harmonized with the roses and other plants near them. From the terrace the lawn continued to the paved walk and plantings on the eastern boundary. Turning to the left, curving borders introduced an informal note farther down, and these with a group of tall trees, including planes and sycamores, gave a certain character of woodland which made a welcome note of informality. The backgrounds were thickened with philadelphus, ribes, brooms, cherries and other flowering shrubs with, in front, proportionally large groups of some of the stronger-growing herbaceous plants and dahlias. The dahlias furnished colour after the shorter flowering period of the herbaceous plants. In the distance between the trees and the long border, the far end was planted with tulips followed by dahlias in glowing scarlet, red and orange, behind dwarf berberis. Seen down the length of the lawn and between the green foliage and dark trunks of the trees, these colours looked very effective. Along the flagged path which followed the northern border, shrubs and plants were chosen which would grow in the shade of the existing trees. Ferns, lilies, berberis and cotoneasters were the main plants with, in the open spaces nearer the buildings, a border of irises interplanted with gladioli. The tennis-courts were placed in a setting of lawn and borders filled with standard cherries, thorns, crab-apples, lilacs and white brooms. Seats in paved recesses in the borders enabled patients to watch the play while staying sheltered.

The Mougin Country Club in the South of France was a favourite resort of Cane's and once, while staying there, he received a message through his host Denet Barry, a director of the club, that the Duke of Connaught would like him to come to lunch and see his gardens. Such an invitation coming from the Duke of Connaught was in the nature of a royal command so needless to say Cane accepted. Cane, though used to much beauty, was astonished at what he found. Branches of white cherries and wistarias all in full bloom combined to make a scene unforgettable in its

A dry walk for the patients at the American Hospital

loveliness. But certain conditions helped to make this loveliness possible. The Duke was in residence for only a comparatively short time each year, and for the remainder of the time the caretakers and gardeners would have had full charge. Cane found his tour round the garden an instance of royal tact. He was walking round with the Duke's equerry Sir Bartley Levett when suddenly at an intersection of paths he found the equerry gone and his place taken by the Duke. Cane remarked how beautifully the plants and flowers were grouped and was told that certain plants, such as wistarias and liliums, were grown in pots and the pots sunk in the soil so that, although they looked natural, really every pot plant had been placed exactly where it would tell most effectively in the general scheme.

At the lunch which followed one of the subjects discussed was art in its various forms, particularly sculpture. Princess Ingrid was there and Cane felt rather pleased with himself because he knew and appreciated the work of Carl Milles, a Swedish sculptor with an international reputation, but one whom no one present other than the Princess and Cane seemed to know of.

Cane was at another luncheon in Cannes at which there was also a princess. This was a German princess and she was the guest of honour. The guests sat waiting for lunch to be served. Time passed and nothing happened. The hostess was obviously becoming uneasy, when the maître d'hôtel, after knocking discreetly at the door and entering, whispered something in her ear. The gist was that because it was just after the war and there was still strong anti-German feeling, the entire kitchen staff had refused to cook for or serve the German princess in any way. Everyone felt sorry for the hostess. However, they lunched off cold ham and salad and had some excellent coffee!

Another celebrity Cane met at Cannes was the German Baroness von Arnem, the author of *Elizabeth and her German Garden* and other works. Cane found her charming but was disappointed that she said so little about her books. Cane had read all of them which made meeting and talking to the author so much more interesting. His recollection of the Baroness was of her sitting on the terrace of her house, surrounded by luxuriant masses of flowers, and of hearing her lively comments on people and things.

Sometimes, when working at Cannes, Cane would go to the golf club-house for the weekend. Often at bank holidays he would motor down to one of the larger hotels and have breakfast on the terrace. This, with scarcely anyone about, was very pleasant. The hotel waiters were attentive, for visitors did not usually get up early at Cannes. Everything—the bright sunshine, the sparkling sea, the whole front swept, washed, and clean—was delightful. After a lazy, enjoyable breakfast under these ideal conditions he would stroll along the main shopping street before motoring on to Monte Carlo for lunch.

Another customer's satisfaction in England led to a job on the Continent. Cane had designed gardens for Clifford Curzon at Highgate, London, and at his Cumberland house. The Curzons also had a place at Litzelburg-am-Attersee in Austria and Cane was asked if he would like to see it.

He accepted the offer and it was the first of several visits to this place on Lake Attersee. The house was delightfully Austrian both in its design and in its furnishing. Cane's bedroom opened onto a roomy balcony from which, looking towards the western end of the lake, the view was a panorama of mountains and lakes enlivened by the sails of an occasional yacht. In the house, wide corridors led to the various rooms and both in corridors and in rooms thick Austrian rugs gave an air of luxurious comfort. The atmosphere too was Austrian, not English; Cane found that being in a cosmopolitan atmosphere enabled him to take broader and sometimes saner views of current questions and to be a more impartial judge of the broad issues of world affairs. The talk there was always stimulating and Cane invariably left the luncheon and dinner table with regret because they had never exhausted the possible avenues of whatever topic was being discussed.

Connecting, as it were, the house with the garden, a wide paved terrace continued from the loggia at the eastern end of the house along the length of the main garden front to return at the western end and lead into the forecourt. From the loggia, where the family usually had an informal Continental breakfast of rolls, butter and tea or coffee, there was a view down the length of a formal terraced garden from which a path meandered to a wooden bridge leading to the boathouse. On the roof of the boathouse one could imagine oneself on the deck of a boat—it was a particularly pleasant place in which to recline in a deckchair and read a book. One could reach the lake from the western end of the house by crossing the lawn then turning, in the rose-garden, to a flight of steps which descended to a lawn glade, its borders on both sides planted with groups of flowering and foliage shrubs, and on to a lake-side terrace. The terrace was paved and partly enclosed by baroque balustrading. A generous seat curved back into the low stone retaining wall. The ground rose at the back behind the wall and seat end and, to give more shelter, groups of low growing berberis and other shrubs were planted behind the wall. On one side the lake terrace was open to a bog-garden. Curzon had made this garden himself; he had planted a number of moisture-loving plants in it. The soil in the border under the house/terrace was comparatively dry and the plants in the lower bog-terrace certainly added to the horticultural interest of the garden as a whole. From this terrace one made one's way following the margin of the lake to the landing-stage and then back to the house.

Apart from music, his gardens comprised Curzon's principal relaxation—though his gardening, Cane found, consisted of planning and planting: he left the digging to others!

Mrs. Curzon was a wonderful organiser and Cane was taken on several trips. Returning to London at one time they went by car to Salzburg where they had booked sleepers on the train but because they went out of their way to look at some historic building they found themselves behind time and had to make a race for it. They made it by the skin of their teeth, clambering aboard with a porter trailing behind with sixteen pieces of luggage. The train was held up long enough to enable the last piece of luggage to be got on board, the porter got his well-deserved tip, and Cane sat back in his seat with a great feeling of relief.

On another occasion when he was staying with the Curzons he decided to go to Vienna, a city he had never visited, for a long weekend before flying back to London. Thinking it would be easy to find accommodation he did nothing about it beforehand and was dismayed to find the city packed. He had visions of having to spend the night in a railway waiting-room, but eventually an official took pity on him and found him a small hotel to stay in. He enjoyed Vienna though he found it colder than he expected: the only place he could really keep warm seemed to be in bed. But he did manage to get a seat for the opera, which pleased him very much.

Another trip abroad for Cane was to Athens where he was to design a garden for President Venezelos. Before he left England he had been given full particulars of the site, with photographs and plans. But though these were very clear and comprehensive Cane felt, as always, that he could not design a garden properly unless he had seen the place and taken in its atmosphere. He had the offer of travelling with the President and his wife who were going by boat from Trieste but excused himself and went by train, the real reason being that he did not want the President to see what a poor sailor he was. But he wished afterwards that he had accepted the invitation for the journey by train was boring; there was no restaurant car and although he had bought bread, cheese, and fruit, the bread, which looked so appetising, was impregnated with whole caraway seeds which he hated. However, the next morning came, and it was fine one; he breakfasted in the hotel at Brindisi and enjoyed the crossing to the port of Athens.

He had hoped that he would have been able to import the plants he wanted for the garden from England, but he found that even the President could not contravene the laws regarding the importation of plants into Greece so he had to rub out his carefully prepared planting plans and begin again. Unfortunately he spoke no Greek and the parks superintendent whom Mme Venezelos had arranged to help him spoke no English. Luckily, however, both had some knowledge of French, so they used that. They went to Athenian nurseries together. Cane made the best use he could of the local material and found the result reasonably satisfactory.

Mme Venezelos insisted that he should see the sights of Athens and gave him a special guide to show him round. He visited the Emanuel Benarki museum, with its fine collection of Byzantine art, the National Museum and, of course, the Acropolis on a moonlight night, to look down through the massive columns of the Parthenon on the shining water of Piraeus, the port of Athens. He liked the city, finding it clean, light, crowded with interesting buildings and immersed in history.

He went to America in 1939 when Sir Louis Beale asked him to do the garden setting for the British Pavilion at the World's Fair in New York. He prepared plans and photographs and took them to Mr. (afterwards Lord) Hudson at the Board of Overseas Trade. He was invited to make suggestions and gave his view that the setting for the pavilion should be something on the lines of the college quadrangles at Oxford and Cambridge. Hudson agreed to this and then asked if Cane could show them some work of his that would give an idea of what he was suggesting for the

Fair. He took them to see Sir John Jarvis's gardens at Hascombe Court, and Hudson and his wife, who had come with him, were suitably impressed. He was told to go ahead with the gardens for the British Pavilion. It was a tricky assignment: to design a garden for anything as important as the World's Fair needed the most careful thought and planning. The garden had to be made as perfect as possible for the opening ceremony and it had to be kept at concert pitch for the duration of the exhibition. As no plants or garden could be at their best for the duration of the Fair, Cane prepared several planting plans. He obtained photographs or sketches of several large trees that were available from gardens or nurseries not too far from the exhibition and on his planting plan he marked the exact spots where he wanted these trees planted and sent the plan in advance to New York so that by the time he arrived there was already the beginning of a garden at the Fair with several mature trees planted and looking as if they really belonged. The gardens had to typify those that form a part of the life of Great Britain.

Cane's basic plan showed all the permanent trees, shrubs and plants. Some of the smaller plants and bulbs had to be lifted before they had finished flowering and their places filled with subjects which would flower later. Sir Louis Beale also arranged for him to have the help of some of the best head gardeners from estates on Long Island, who grew the plants ready to be moved into their allotted spaces when required. To do this required precise organisation but it did pay for the extra trouble as by this means the borders were full for the whole of the flowering season. So that the garden always appeared as an exhibition garden should, the actual work of changing the plants was carried out in the early morning before the Fair was open to the public. It all worked smoothly, thanks largely to willing co-operation on the part of Mr. Pierpoint Morgan and the other head gardeners and Cane's own foreman who was there for something like a year and a half.

The British Pavilion was erected on a bare piece of ground, a fragment of the vast space that had formerly been the rubbish dump for the city of New York. The garden occupied a site of over three-quarters of an acre and was designed as a long rectangle leading into a semi-circle.

Cane was disappointed that he was not able to stay for the opening ceremony but the New York papers were carrying alarming headlines forecasting imminent war for Britain; also, the *Queen Mary* was about to sail so Cane, worried about his staff and practice in London, decided to return on her.

A description of the garden in the British Pavilion at the New York World's Fair was published in *Country Life* of 9 December 1939. Written by G. C. Taylor it said that it had been carried out with conspicuous skill by Percy Cane, and that it was typically English but in keeping with the main facade of the pavilion. The report continued:

> . . . it is designed as a plain rectangle sweeping unbroken into a semi-circle at its farthest end . . . the central portion an unbroken stretch of mown turf which gives to the garden a feeling of spaciousness and quiet beauty—qualities which are essentially English. A flagged path—the stones of which came from Whitehall Gardens and the Tower of London—borders the lawn and emphasises the formal lines of the design at the same time providing a dry walk round the garden.
>
> Being designed as a private garden, dense green walls of thuya were planted to ensure privacy—another English quality—while pines and birches with all the air of the English countryside find a place within the hedges, heightening the effect of seclusion and permanence and throwing into relief the glowing colours of drifts, of tulips in the spring which were followed later by bold groups of hardy flowers, affording another typical English feature—the herbaceous border. These arranged in a series of harmonious colours changing from soft pinks through blues and mauves to strong reds and yellows afforded a striking display along the whole length of the borders. Thousands of lily bulbs . . . planted in generous colonies afforded picturesque incidents and bright splashes of colour among the azaleas and cherries in the semi-circular area, reflecting the increasing popularity of this aristocratic group of hardy bulbs.
>
> Ornamental flowering trees and shrubs of various kinds all added to the effect of the garden in different seasons and were so placed that each contributed to the design. The vista through birches with the underplanting of heather, reminding one of a Surrey common is such as only an English garden can provide and it says much for the skill and ingenuity of the designer that such charming and picturesque incidents were achieved in spite of the inhospitable morass when it was taken in hand and the trying restrictions in the choice of plants. In its simple and straightforward design which shows the happy concord now existing between the formal and natural schools, in the quiet spaciousness of the mown lawn with birches and pines rising from its level surface, in the

richly coloured ribbon of herbaceous flowers and in the old sundial the garden provided a harmonious and typically English setting for the Pavilion as well as selecting that strong measure of individuality which is characteristic of most of our garden efforts.

The World's Fair garden was situated in an area bordered by the American Horticultural Society's gardens, separated from it only by a hedge. Mrs. Harriett Pratt, the President of the Society, came to Cane one day and told him she was aware that something was wrong with the Society's gardens and could he tell them what it was? Cane, feeling flattered, suggested one or two slight alterations which were carried out in accordance with his suggestions. But, though Cane did not say so as he was a visitor and also because Mrs. Pratt was a charming woman, whom he liked, he would have re-designed the gardens completely for to him the basic idea or design was not a good one. But he kept his opinion to himself.

A regular visitor to Cane's Buckinghamshire home at Upper Spur-lands was Colonel Charley, a man who transacted business in the United Kingdom for Haile Selassie, the Emperor of Ethiopia. Charley was an admirer of Cane's garden designing and so it was natural that when he learned that the Emperor was looking for someone to design gardens for a new palace at Addis Ababa he should recommend Cane.

Plans of the palace—the work of a French architect Edouard Perret—were sent to Cane to study. Cane then flew to Addis Ababa several times to supervise the making of the gardens.

The new palace dominated the city and- yet, enclosed within its surrounding gardens and woods, was very private. The city itself was a mixture of the old and the new: small one-storey shops not much more than thatched huts contrasted with modern buildings rising all around. The palace stood more or less centrally in its own grounds, on elevated land. It was sumptuous in design and Cane realised that any gardens he made would have to fit in with this. The site for the gardens when Cane first saw it was a rough, exposed piece of rocky ground dotted here and there with native dwellings. He realised that the situation of the palace gave an opportunity for gardens entirely different in character on its eastern and western fronts. On the eastern front the ground fell gradually to the eastern boundary while to the west a steep fall made terraces and stairways necessary in any design. The principal entrance to which the main drives

The entrance drives to the Imperial Palace at Addis Ababa, Ethiopia

led was on the mildly sloping eastern side. So here level lawns and a gravelled forecourt made a suitable setting for the classical elevations of the palace. Cane has always maintained that entrance drives should not be gardens but that they should be so designed that their formality contrasts with the gardens' more luxuriant trees, flowers and colours, throwing them into higher relief. In addition, it was necessary to give these entrance drives at Addis Ababa a spacious and dignified setting that would be a fitting approach to the stately elevations of the new palace. It was also necessary to make provision for parking cars for receptions and other functions. To meet these requirements Cane devised two parallel drives separated by a proportionately wide stretch of turf, one for vehicles coming in and one for those going out. The long lines of the drives in a rich green setting of mown turf and conifers made the approach both spacious and dignified.

Central on the principal entrance across the level forecourt, wide shallow steps were made to lead to a long water-garden with fountains playing and with the pool flanked by columnar conifers. This led to another forecourt and a rose-garden at the lower part of the grounds. When it was ready it was possible for someone to stand on the steps of the highest terrace and watch the fountains throwing water—iridescent in the sunshine—against a background of water-lilies. Cane then felt that he had succeeded in providing a fit setting for an imperial palace.

(In his original plan Cane had shown a classical shelter but it tended to block a fine view of the palace from the water-garden—a view that Haile Selassie was very fond of—so Cane had it removed from the plans.)

Other vistas were constructed. One gave a view down the length of the water-gardens to car drivers turning to enter the forecourt with, between these formal water-gardens and the conifers (Chamaecyparis) that flanked the drives, a winding glade of flowering trees and shrubs, the vivid colours of the flowers showing an almost tropical brilliance against their dark background of firs. Another vista, close to and parallel with the eastern boundary, extended the length of the gardens from north to south through the rose-garden to a terrace on the western boundary with conifers at regular intervals to emphasise the length and importance of the vista. The western elevation of the palace opened onto a wide terrace built in natural rock high above the lower garden. The rock wall was almost vertical and wide flights of steps were built from it to the gardens with two symmetrical balustraded stairways leading to the lowest landing. From a loggia in the wall at the back of the landing a wide flight of steps descended to garden level. In these lower gardens the central lawn extended between groups of evergreen and flowering shrubs to a natural pool near the western boundary and from this lawn, glades, formed between plantations, swept round to a long straight walk connecting the eastern and western gardens. On the north side a tennis-court was screened by trees and shrubs and a formal flower-garden bordered the paved walks. From the formal terrace on the southern boundary, there were lovely views to the river below.

The formal water-gardens and a long, straight walk through a rose-garden on to a plain formal terrace on the south boundary together extended the formal design to the limits of the gardens. Banks of trees and shrubs flanking lawn glades, and giving vistas of colour, and specimen trees, separately and in groups, rose from the mown turf. The gardens were thus varied in interest—lovely both in themselves and as a setting for the palace.

On one of Cane's first journeys to Addis Ababa he flew first to Nairobi as he wanted to contact a well-known nursery near the city. At this nursery he was able to get a great deal of useful information as to what plants, shrubs, and trees would grow successfully in the Addis Ababa area of Ethiopia. While in Nairobi he was taken round the game reserve and was particularly intrigued with the lions which came round his car. The mayor of Nairobi told him that one day he had found a fully grown lioness sitting comfortably on the doorstep of his office and had had to call a keeper to escort the lioness back to where she belonged. On another journey to Addis Ababa, Cane stopped off at Cairo for a whole day. He liked Cairo especially as he had V.I.P. treatment: Mr. Whitney Straight had asked officials of B.O.A.C. to entertain him. This entertainment included a visit to the pyramids, which meant walking through long narrow tunnels, standing in the centre of the pyramid and gazing up through an aperture like a narrow chimney, with roughly hewn sides and a small hole at the top. Cane wondered what the chimney-sweep boys of olden times would have thought of it. They would at least have appreciated the fact that there was no soot! Offered a ride on a camel, Cane refused. He found the camel a high, disdainful and supercilious-looking animal with the power to make human beings feel small and insignificant. Getting back to his hotel after an enjoyable day Cane was told that there would be no plane flying to Addis Ababa the following morning. This gave him another day in Cairo so he went first to the Tutankhamun Museum and found himself transported back centuries, right into the life and art of one of the oldest civilisations; and in the afternoon he visited a mosque where, changing his shoes for slippers, he entered the vast building with its quality rugs scattered over the whole floor.

While Cane was in Ethiopia the Emperor asked for his advice on a place for a game reserve, so early one morning he set off accompanied by the city architect. They breakfasted on the way on a wide terrace overlooking a magnificent view and Cane says that he has never found coffee and rolls taste as good as on that occasion. Travelling by way of an extremely rough road they reached their destination by midday. It was a lovely spot, quiet and peaceful. The smooth surface of a lake lay calm and unruffled stretching away into the distance. On the far shore, a rather mangy looking lion and lioness were already in residence. So, too, were monkeys and other animals including, loveliest of all, a flock of flamingoes, their white plumage shining like snow in the sunshine. The lake was beautifully situated, undisturbed except for these animals which would form the basis of a game reserve. The place appeared entirely suitable for the suggested purpose and Cane and the city architect reported so on their return. Apart from the wonderful scenery and the animals, Cane's deepest other recollection of the journey was feeling sore for several days afterwards as a result of the travelling.

5
Gardens of One's Own

About 1935 Cane had a longing for country life again, as a change from living in London. He considered the matter carefully. His work was based in London which was very convenient, for from nowhere else could he so easily make his frequent journeys all over Britain and abroad. He decided to have a cottage not far from London but in the end bought a little dairy-farm at Holmer Green near Beaconsfield in Buckinghamshire and re-christened the place with what he understood had been its former name, Upper Spurlands.

Upper Spurlands, small and unpretentious, was seventeenth century. Its beams were part of the original building and nothing was false about it. That was why Cane liked it, for his taste was for plain, straightforward houses with good proportions in their rooms, Georgian or Georgian-Italian in character. But Upper Spurlands had quite definitely its own character: possibly it could be described as 'English Farmhouse' if there were such an architectural designation.

Cane was delighted to become the possessor of a house and land enough to feel himself in a small way the owner of a tiny estate. He enjoyed walking round the perimeter. The property consisted of the farmhouse, a large barn, several cow sheds and pig sties and about twenty-five acres of land, chiefly pasture. House and buildings stood back some distance from the road. There were two separate self-contained meadows as well as other, smaller enclosures, one of which, comparatively long and narrow, was 1,000 feet in length, started from the front of the house and ran at right angles to the far boundary. This strip of land varied from fifty to a hundred feet in width and was enclosed with thorn hedges; Cane decided to turn it into a garden. But he soon realised that it was rather too ambitious a project and that the garden would be out of scale with the house. It would be a garden for a small mansion tacked on to a cottage. He thought he could correct that by adding a fair-sized sitting-room, with a bedroom and bathroom over it, to the house. As it was, the house contained a comfortable sitting-room, a dining-room, a kitchen, a small scullery and a dairy on the ground floor with two good bedrooms and, opening from a small separate landing, two single rooms. The bathroom was at the bottom of the hall on the ground floor. The house was large enough to be a pleasant little weekend retreat with comfortable accommodation for one or two friends.

It was certainly countrified. Cane took his London housekeeper down to see it one day and after she had looked over it he asked her how she liked the kitchen.

'What kitchen?' was the housekeeper's abrupt reply.

'The one behind the dining-room, of course'.

'Oh', she said, 'you mean the scullery with the pump and the big stone sink!'

But later on when Cane moved back into a rather larger flat in London he had great difficulty in persuading her to return though she was a Londoner by birth and upbringing.

As for the gardens of Upper Spurlands, they were in a desolate state when Cane took over. Thistles grew as high as his shoulders in what should have been the kitchen-garden, and in fact it was some time before Cane realised he had such a garden: only by exploring did he become aware that his small estate included anything as useful as this was to prove to be. He came to realise that the deserted kitchen-garden was rather a charming corner. In it were several apple trees, their trunks old and gnarled and infested it seemed with the eggs and larvae of all the enemies to good, clean fruit. But Cane liked the shape of these old trees and he got them cleaned, pruned and sprayed after which they produced quite respectable crops of apples.

Over the rest of the estate the land was poor, the hedges were overgrown, whitethorns encroached on what Cane had earmarked to be the main feature of the garden—the long glade—and there was a general air of neglect over the whole place.

But through it all he recognised the charm and potential beauty of the place. It appealed to him just as much as if it had been in perfect condition. Just scything the weeds made a tremendous difference. He turned the mare which, though not being an expert horseman he liked riding, out into one of the paddocks to eat the grass. Next he put cows to join her in the job. Both

Percy Cane's own garden in the country at Upper Spurlands, Holmer Green, Buckinghamshire

mare and cows ate the grass, but unfortunately, naturally left all the thistles and docks standing. So these had to be chopped down or dug up by hand.

He made a three-year plan for the garden. From making this garden he quickly learned one valuable lesson. To begin with, he thought that if he gave his regular gardener extra help the work would get done easily and economically. But he found this was not so. There was, he soon discovered, a marked difference between the work of making gardens professionally and the routine work of a gardener, and however good an ordinary gardener was at his own job, to employ him in making a garden was not an economical proposition. So Cane brought a working foreman from his London headquarters to give the gardener extra help and hoped that the two would get on. Which they did: they liked working together and everything turned out for the best. The gardener also looked after the livestock. This man, George Smith, knew exactly how to handle cows and pigs, and knew that he knew. The one thing he did not like was working late. He would stay until eight as a special favour if it was really necessary but nothing would induce him to stay after that. Usually it did not matter but when the cow was taken ill and had to be milked during the night as well as the usual time, George refused to turn out and Cane had to get up

The rose-garden at Upper Spurlands

between one and two in the morning and milk the cow himself. He continued to do this night after night and though he went back to bed again after milking he always seemed to be tired; this gave him a sympathy with farm workers that he would otherwise never have had. George, the so-called gardener—he was really a stockman and had come to Cane because he wanted to be a gardener—'looked as much at home when attending to the cows and pigs as he appeared to be lost in the garden. He was a good-natured sort and put up with my scanty knowledge of cows and pigs and their requirements with a sort of pitying look on his face, an expression that said plainly that little was to be expected from anyone who came from London and who, in his opinion, plainly belonged there'.

To return to the garden. In it the borders were wide enough to grow a comprehensive collection of flowering shrubs, each shrub standing separately so that it could develop and really show its shape in full beauty. A grove of Prunus (cherries) came next to laburnums (*L. vossii*) with their long racemes of yellow flowers like curtains hanging over the white flowers of *Viburnum mariesii*; the yellow of the laburnums against the white background was a beautiful sight. White-flowered lilacs were also lovely with their opulent masses of blooms against the yellow laburnums. Red and purple lilacs toned in with rhododendrons and though lilacs like lime these did not seem to mind the masses of peat which Cane added to the soil before planting the rhododendrons. It might have been the shelter from wind, or it might have been the deep cultivation, Cane never knew, but the rhododendrons he planted when quite small lived to grow into fine specimens. Filling the saucer-shaped hollows in which they were planted with peat or decaying leaf mould, to which was added an occasional dusting of bonemeal, kept them in fine health.

After the gardens were finished Cane used to hold an annual garden party each July to keep in touch with his friends; he says he cannot remember ever having a really fine day for one of these parties. To help him entertain, his cousin, the wife of Dr. Elliott, who lived only a few miles away, acted as hostess. The guests, however, did not mind overmuch what the weather was like for they enjoyed coming into the dining-room with its heavy beams and cavernous fireplace and in July, with a blazing log fire, the table pushed to one side to serve as a kind of bar counter, a wide variety of drinks (tea was served in the sitting-room) and plenty of cigarettes, the garden was soon forgotten. One year Cane opened the garden for the Queen's Nurses' Fund. During the afternoon Cane was looking at something in one of the borders when a visitor came up to him and asked him if he really thought the gardens were worth the entrance fee of half a crown. Cane mumbled something about the good of the cause and moved away. The questioner did not know who he was. Cane did feel that it was well worth the money for he had been to several other gardens which had been opened to the public in this way and he considered his own garden was just as good as these. The glade was lovely, full of well-arranged colour; the rose-garden a little past its best, but taking everything into consideration he really felt that his own garden was something to be proud of.

One of the great pleasures Cane found from living in the country was that he could keep pets and give them a freedom that was impossible in town life. At Spurlands he had a pedigree cocker bitch, which one day presented him with a litter of puppies from which he chose two to keep. One, which he named Sinner, was a handsome dog who held his head high as if he were proud of himself and had feathered legs and charming manners. The other was a golden bitch with a temperament the exact opposite of Sinner's. She was disobedient, would not be trained, and ran after people; her only redeeming feature was her lovely silky golden coat. Cane decided to keep just Sinner and gave the other to his secretary. Sinner was a one-man dog and very faithful to Cane. He had an engaging trait of sitting behind his master on the back of the chair when there were guests for lunch or dinner and of watching the proceedings from this vantage-point. At what he considered the right time he would get down and go round the table, stopping at each person's chair to look up with his soulful eyes to see what he might expect in the way of bones or other tidbits. Having made the round of the table and having assured himself that there was nothing else to be got he insinuated himself again on the back of the chair and watched the proceedings again, always from under his master's right arm. Sinner was usually fed in the kitchen and the sincerest test of his affection was that he would, after looking at the door and weighing things up, choose to stay in the dining-room with his master while his own dinner was waiting for him in the kitchen.

By the time he went to Upper Spurlands Cane had entered journalism again—this time as a publisher and editor with his own periodical which came out in spring 1930 as *GARDEN DESIGN, Landscape, Architecture, Horticulture,* from 2 Westminster Palace Gardens, S.W.1. The first editorial stated:

> In editing a new periodical on garden design and horticulture I should like to give briefly my reasons for thinking that it will fulfil a definite need and will be welcomed.
>
> It is recognised that Great Britain is pre-eminently the home of gardens. Garden making has been practised from time immemorial and design in this country has been influenced to a considerable degree by that of the continental gardens, especially the best of those in Italy, France and Holland. We have, however, evolved a style of our own and there is, in the fine gardens of Great Britain, a rich interweaving of formal and informal design that is not to be found elsewhere. We have in the art of garden making a reputation both to uphold and to enhance . . .
>
> Gardens should be proportional in extent to, and entirely in harmony with, the style and character of the house for which they form the setting and in the case of the more expensive ones, they should be happily related to the surrounding landscape. These fundamentals of design and

A Percy Cane garden at the Chelsea Show

proportion are, more often than not, entirely ignored. The big opportunity is seldom developed and most gardens are small in their conception, spoiled by fussy detail and only made interesting by the flowers and plants with which they are filled.

Among its contributors over the years appeared the names of such writers as A. T. Johnson, R. F. Notcutt, Constance Spry, G. S. Thomas, W. E. Shewell-Cooper, Eleanour Sinclair Rohde, Hilda M. Smith, Clarence Elliott, R. B. Dawson and N. P. Harvey. And Cane himself contributed to most issues with both signed and unsigned articles, mainly on garden design and accompanied by illustrations of gardens he had created or was creating. The periodical continued as a quarterly for nine years. The spring 1939 issue was retitled *House and Garden Design* and the editorial stated that from the next number the journal would be enlarged to deal more fully with architecture and interior decoration.

In a competition age, nothing but the best has any hope of survival, and it will be the aim of editor and publishers alike to maintain and enhance the value of a magazine which has always tried to make its angle of approach as wide as possible to the garden-loving public.

But this was the last issue to appear.

Many of Cane's clients came as a result of recommendations from other customers. Many more approached him at the Chelsea Show. Living at home in the country about fifty miles from London Cane, as a young man, had been scarcely aware of such important events as the shows of the Royal Horticultural Society. Then he paid a visit to London to the Great Spring Show of the R.H.S. and this was a revelation to him of what a show should be. As a result of this visit Cane determined to exhibit a garden at the nearest local show: it was the horticultural section of the Essex Agricultural Society's show at Chelmsford. He had no plants or flowers with which to make his exhibit but nothing daunted he managed to persuade nurseries to let him have what he wanted. Even a small garden like this was an innovation and his efforts were crowned with success, winning a medal for him. This was the beginning of showing both locally and at Chelsea.

The shows at Chelsea had only recently started up again after World War I when Cane began showing. In 1921 he had designs and photographs in the special Artists' Tent at the hospital end of the ground. His business address was given as 67/68 Broad Street Arcade, E.C.2. From then onwards Cane appeared every year at Chelsea. The location of his exhibit varied a little: in 1924 it was in the Main Avenue, from 1926 to 1928 'in the Art Tent in the Ranelagh Gardens' and in 1929 'in the Art Tent on the Lawn'. In 1931, besides plans and photographs he showed a model of a garden. In 1932 the exhibitors of plans, sketches and photographs of gardens became so numerous as to require a special section of the tent under 'Garden Design Tent', where they displayed block plans and colour-wash plans of the gardens they had designed, and often supplemented them with enlarged photography. But it soon became evident to Cane that the tent was in rather a backwater and that more business went to the exhibitors of actual gardens and plants.

So in 1934, against no doubt well-meant advice, Cane showed his first proper garden at Chelsea. Again he had no nursery on which to draw for shrubs and plants but he was able to get more or less what he wanted. At this, his first attempt, he was awarded a silver-gilt medal. His showing seemed to coincide with the breaking away from the very formal gardens

which had previously been such a feature of Chelsea. The *Gardeners Chronicle*, in reporting on this show, said:

> . . . the exhibitors of formal gardens used much less masonry than in many other years and the gardens gained immensely in attraction. Nearly all were gardens and not architectural erections: friendly, homely gardens which the owner could tend and enjoy. This does not mean that the mason was banished entirely from the garden. His valuable aid is often enlisted in the laying of the York paving which permits one to stroll around in all weathers: in the building of boundary walls: for corner garden houses . . .

And it went on to say of Cane's particular effort:

> Percy Cane favours wide borders of sombre conifers lightened with red-leaved Japanese maples and mauve rhododendrons, set in ample greensward leading to a heather-thatched house.

The following year, which was the Silver Jubilee of the R.H.S., Cane laid out a broad border with a hedge of tall cypresses and filled it with specimen conifers and large massed pink rhododendrons. Next to the broad border there was a winding lawn and more conifers margined with blue violas, white azaleas and, beyond, pink rhododendrons. Behind this border a paved path led to a heather-thatched summer-house. Once again Cane was awarded a silver-gilt medal. The 1936 show was held in good weather and was acclaimed one of the best of all time. That year some of the sites at the Embankment end were allotted to rock gardens so this cut down on the number of formal gardens. The term 'formal', however, was becoming a misnomer in many cases for though for convenience' sake all these self-contained gardens were described as 'formal', some were distinctly informal although none-the-less very attractive. Cane once again used a heather-thatched summer-house as a focal point in a corner of the paved terrace of his garden and from it was a view of the spacious lawn and borders of Japanese maples and various azaleas. But he had evidently learnt from his experience of the previous two years for this time he received a gold medal which was to be the first of many.

The following year he received another gold medal together with a

Opposite, top: A Percy Cane garden at Chelsea
Opposite, bottom: A Percy Cane garden at Chelsea

A Percy Cane garden at Chelsea

Coronation Cup in silver-gilt given to each exhibitor who got a gold medal, in commemoration of the accession of George VI. The *Gardeners Chronicle* described his garden thus:

> Charm and an air of refinement were the characteristic of Percy Cane's garden, entrance to which was obtained through a tall hedge of *Cupressus lawsoniana* approached by a broad sweep of turf. Against the hedge were large banks of low-growing conifers. The garden within was of formal design with a heather-thatched summer-house and a lawn bounded by broad, paved walls. The borders were bright with azaleas, irises and Japanese maples underplanted with violas and there was also a fountain pool of attractive design.

The heather-thatched summer-house seems to have gone by the next year when Cane received a gold medal for a garden with turf in the middle and broad, winding borders planted chiefly with large prostrate junipers, cypresses, pines and yews with, at one part, a delightful planting of rich blue gentians and some liliums. The 1939 show, which was to be the last for several years, was a show remembered chiefly for the dismal weather rather than for the variety and beauty of the exhibits, for during the show the wind howled and brought chilliness from the north, the rain fell in torrents night and day and the surfaces of the outside paths and roads were reduced to thin liquid mud. Nevertheless, Queen Mary, who had only missed one Chelsea Show (in 1912), braved the elements on the Tuesday and with umbrella up even visited many of the exhibits outside the big tent. Cane's exhibit, perhaps in keeping with the weather and the threat of war, was more sombre than usual although it was relieved by white walls and occasional little groups of liliums among large spreading junipers and cedars. The judges evidently thought highly of it for they awarded him a silver cup.

When showing started again after the war representatives of the Royal Horticultural Society telephoned Cane to ask if he would take two plots instead of the usual one. After some consideration Cane agreed but only on the understanding that he could use them to make one garden. The garden when completed was the largest of the laid-out gardens at Chelsea in its 1947 show. It was more informal than the pre-war gardens had been. Effective use was made of *Pinus cembra* whose fresh growths appeared like pale green plumes against darker, older foliage. Azaleas planted in blocks

Percy Cane as a young man

of single colours and edged with violas in similar drifts. The banks of colour were relieved occasionally by low, spreading junipers. The garden was bordered by *Cupressus fletcherii* and tall *Cupressus lawsoniana*. Many of the pines and azaleas hid their smaller companions from view until one drew close and thus the scene changed considerably with the aspect. In the two far corners were a well and garden seat chiselled in stone. This 1947 Chelsea was remarkable for its extent and beauty especially as traders were only just emerging from the difficulties imposed by a prolonged war. Once again Cane was awarded a gold medal.

The promise of 1947 came to fruition in the following year and the formal and informal gardens were even better than before with those responsible showing good taste and a great variety of design. To quote the *Gardeners Chronicle* show report once again:

> Percy Cane again made admirable use of his space. In the limited space he succeeded by skilful plotting to give the impression of distance and also provided several very delightful vistas. The general scheme was of sweeping curved lawns bordered by generous plantings of pink and red rhododendrons edged with spreading little conifers and ericas with a background of tall cypresses. At one side a York-stone path led to a dignified restful place, also well-laid with paving, bordered with large shapely conifers and containing a desirable well-head and carved stone seats. Excellent plants of *Lilium regale* provided the touches of near-white without which, they tell us, no garden scheme can be complete.

This garden brought a gold medal as did the one for 1949 which was skilfully designed to combine the formal and the informal. It had a surround of high conifers and the focal point was a carved stone well-head with a small trim lawn in the foreground. The informal part was screened with specimen conifers and planted with brilliant azaleas and other shrubs with borders of liliums and beds of bearded irises.

A break in gold medals came in the following year when a silver-gilt was the award for a garden which achieved a spacious effect with a skilful combination of the formal and informal bounded once again with a hedge of conifers. On one side fine specimen rhododendrons were well blended and included *R. dido*, the crimson Vanguard and the pink Mrs. Shirley. A lily-pool with a stone pedestal surmounted by a metal figure was flanked by beds of irises, in pale colours, while deeper shades were planted in front of the conifers. An irregular bed displayed rhododendrons, acers, cypresses and azaleas while liliums and conifers were extensively grouped on the lawn. But it was back to a gold medal in 1951 for a garden which had a formal stone garden-house looking out on a pool and large lawn. Around

The lake and woods are the principal motif for the garden at The Aviary, Southall

the garden were large specimen rhododendrons, acers, and azaleas in association with ericas and liliums. Another successful year followed but in 1953 Cane decided that with the increasing costs of putting on a garden at Chelsea, and also because by now he was getting enough recommended work to keep him busy, he would just show plans, photographs and sketches and be on hand to discuss things with his clients once again. So back he went to the Garden Design Tent where he received many a Grenfell medal for his exhibits of gardens and plans and photographs.

Cane's method of working was to pay an initial visit himself to every client during which he would get the feel of the place and receive any special instructions. A survey would then be made by the drawing-room staff and a plan of the garden, as it then was, made. On this plan Cane would then prepare a design or designs, and planting plans, which would then be discussed with the client and any amendments made. An estimate of costs would then be drawn up in the office or, if the work were to be carried out by a contractor, detailed plans would be sent to two or three firms so that they could prepare estimates for the work. These contractors would be located as near the job as possible.

At one time Cane had twelve to fourteen foremen who would be sent to the jobs and they would engage any additional labour they required locally. But over the years these foremen left and with the increasing cost of labour the work tended to be carried out more and more by local contractors. There was more fluidity among the drawing-office and other inside staff, with a good deal of coming and going. Also, from time to time, Cane took articled pupils who did a two-year course. A considerable number of nurseries were used and these tended to be treated as specialists in certain types of plants. He joined the Institute of Landscape Architects at one period but later fell out with them over the interpretation of some of the rules and resigned. He was always very much of a lone worker and did not have a great deal to do with others in his profession.

The Royal Horticultural Society awarded Cane the Veitch Memorial Gold Medal in 1963 for his services to horticulture and as recognition of his work as a designer of gardens and a landscape architect. The Veitch award is made 'to those who have helped in the advancement and improvement of the science and practice of horticulture'.

Part of the park at Woburn Abbey in Bedfordshire

6
Writing about Gardens

Although Cane had contributed many articles and plans for magazines early in his career, it was not until 1926 that his first book was published. Geoffrey Holme, who edited *The Studio* art magazine, asked him to write the text for a book *Modern Gardens British and Foreign*. He was given photographs from which to make a selection. The book, which came out as a special winter number of *The Studio* 1926-7, was edited by Geoffrey Holme and Shirley B. Wainwright. As well as twenty-four pages of introduction by Cane it contained illustrations of gardens designed by him at Little Bowden, Pangbourne, and Kingswood House, Sunningdale. Among other British garden architects featured were Milner, Son and White, Avray Tipping, Wratten and Godfrey, Romaine-Walker and Jenkins, Farquarson, Oliver Hill, Braddell and Deane, Dawber, Baillie Scott and Beresford, Douglas Wells, Evelyn Cowell, Falconer, Baker and Campbell, and Wontner Smith. Gardens included in the book came from Great Britain, America, France, Germany, Austria, Italy, Sweden, Denmark and Japan.

Some years later, in 1934, Cane was asked to write a book of his own, the title to be *Garden Design of Today*. The subject appealed to him and he willingly acceded to the request. He enjoyed writing this book more than the previous one for he felt he was now more master of his subject. It dealt particularly with the artistic side of garden planning and making. Two chief threads were interwoven through the various chapters: first, the elementary laws of design, and secondly, practical information to help towards their successful application. Cane gave his views on the most suitable treatment for various kinds of gardens, so that the readers would be able to recognise the possibilities of any particular site and so develop them in the most suitable way. The history of garden design and horticulture was touched on but only insofar as it had a bearing on modern design. The book gave little comparison between the different so-called

A glade shown to advantage at The Old Parsonage, Marlow, Buckinghamshire

'styles' but attempted to show that each could be right and beautiful in its results. If there was a keynote running through the book it was that the special character of any site should be developed in the most effective way, without too much regard for rules and styles. If any particular form of design was stressed (as in the chapter on Japanese gardens) it was because of some inherent value that was of general application.

The gardens of which descriptions were given were chosen to illustrate solutions to certain problems of planning springing from some unusual features of particular sites.

One reviewer of the book, in remarking on the fact that the keynote was that every site should be treated on its own special merits or special character, and its special features developed as effectively as possible without regard for preconceived rules, said that this recalled to him Capability Brown who, after inspecting a proposed new site for a garden, always asserted that 'it has its capabilities'.

*Paved terrace in a garden surrounded by mature trees at Hillside, Four Oaks,
Warwickshire*

It was twenty-two years before Cane wrote his next book, *The Earth is my Canvas,* published in 1956. The title was suggested to him by C. S. Claverley, manager of the Kent Oil Refinery at the Isle of Grain in Kent when he was designing the gardens for the refinery. This book dealt more particularly with gardens that Cane had designed and made, the problem or problems encountered in each case and the solutions he had given, together with, as far as possible, his reasons for the suggested treatment. The book was well received. *Country Life* wrote that 'he [Cane] seems as much in demand for making and re-making as Lancelot Brown was in his day and, seeing that "Distance is no object" as the furniture removers' vans rather puzzlingly announce, he gets farther afield than Capability ever dreamed of.' *Ideal Home* said that he had achieved his reputation 'as much by his exercise of restraint as by other virtues and has consistently been able to avoid the all-too-common fault of over designing and over planting'. And the *Royal Horticultural Society Journal* added that 'Mr. Cane clearly has a wonderful gift of making the most of a site', but went to to say that 'withal it has to be conceded that this is a book of dreams, a dream of beauty from the past but dreams not likely to be realised again in the future. The noble vistas, the far-reaching terraces, the wandering glades, the broad borders of Mr. Cane's creation can have no place in the gardens of tomorrow . . . Changed economic circumstances will make every man his own garden-architect and he will do well to study the best in the past. In this spirit he may turn to Mr. Cane's book'.

But the pessimism of the *R.H.S. Journal* reviewer was not borne out and Cane became busier than ever as the years went by. Yet he was very conscious of the changes that had to be made with the increasing cost of labour and maintenance. At a symposium in which he took part in 1957 with two other landscape architects, Brenda Colvin and L. Milner White, he said:

Economy seems to be the order of the day and we must try and combine utility and beauty in the most satisfying way. Flowering trees and shrubs instead of bedding plants. Do not have a rock garden. Have paved paths if costs allow. Have a small formal garden as a contrast to the glades and informal walks. If a large garden, why not turn part of it into a woodland with walks of turf or heather. Silver birches are good: rhododendrons and azaleas if soil is right. The art of making a small garden appear larger than it is lies in having everything, trees, groups of shrubs, separate gardens, proportional to the extent of the garden as a whole. Whereas straight lines and boundaries tend to reduce size, curving borders or trees and shrubs, skilfully managed, can be made to give an illusion of much greater distance than actually is.

The next book, *The Creative Art of Garden Design,* was something in the nature of a résumé of the many places he had designed during his years of practice as a garden architect. It also endeavoured to explain how the many problems that arose might be dealt with. Published in 1967, it contained over seventy illustrations of gardens and plans. The *Times Educational Supplement* said of it:

> The result . . . may not in general be for the likes of us . . . but the principles are the same. Anyway we can all take pleasure in the beauty of it all, the product of what Mr. Cane terms 'the relation of the different parts that together make up the whole and the loveliness of its colour harmonies'.

And *House and Garden* described the book as:

> . . . basically a series of analyses and explanations of the reasons underlying a group of gardens designed by Cane, many of them now famous. The text is amplified by photographs of gardens which apparently owe little to any strongly held convictions of naturalism versus formalism, trees versus flowers, statuary versus shrubs. Cane is the most eclectic of garden designers, a fact well illustrated by a group of diagrams which conclude the book. These designs are likely to be of considerable interest to more modest gardeners for they answer urban and suburban problems as readily as his photographs indicate that he has dealt with the larger problems of great estates.

Cane was always attracted to writing and though he loved designing he often wondered whether or not he would have got the same amount of pleasure from his work had he been solely a professional creative writer. He found words interesting to play with and even when turned ninety he was trying his hand at a new writing form (for him)—a novel.

His writing was always of a very high standard and he always had the ability to express himself clearly and concisely on the most intricate details of garden design and of similar subjects. The following extracts from his books and magazines will give some idea of the quality and range of his work. The extracts are arranged alphabetically.

AMERICA

. . . has problems and difficulties to overcome by reason of her history as a world power and her immense size as a continent, which in the case of other great nations have been a matter of evolution through long periods of time. Instead of originating the national arts she has searched the world and fed aesthetically from those of other countries. On finding that inspiration drawn from these sources is not always the best and most suitable to her needs, she has demolished and built again, and if necessary again demolished and again rebuilt; but all the time her own personality is assimilating and progressing towards the perfecting of a national style. Just as in other countries garden design has waited on domestic architecture, so in America the importance of the garden setting is now realised . . .

As one would expect in so vast a country, horticulture and garden design are influenced to a marked degree by climatic and local conditions with considerable diversity, as a consequence, both in the character of design and planting.—*Modern Gardens*

ATMOSPHERE

This atmosphere of a garden or site is really . . . something intangible, to which everything—trees, contours, the architectural character of the house, the presence of water or rock, and the surroundings all contribute. I have seen a single pine or a group of pine trees so beautiful in outline that one instinctively felt that the scheme of the garden must be subordinated, and lead the eye to them as the principal feature.—*Modern Gardens*

AUTUMN

. . . makes us more aware of the deceitfulness of distance because already the colours seen close up, without any perspective whatever, are changing. It is the year's *âge dangereuse* and any exaggeration may be expected in the way of its demonstrating how beautiful and gay and unconquerable it is. And as all right-minded persons will forgive a charming woman any folly and grieve seriously when the flame falls to dust, so we applaud the brave show of the ageing year, and as long as it has any voice to challenge us, we reply, 'I think you are delightful as you are'.—*Garden Design*, Autumn 1936

AXIAL LINES

A necessary preliminary to planning is the laying down of vistas, and axial lines, on which these are built, must, so to speak, form the skeleton of the design. The positions of such lines are not always obvious, and require great nicety of judgement in their selection, but so important are they that the whole design can be either made or marred by their placing. When the reverse is the case, and separate gardens are indiscriminately pieced together, there must result a restless lack of unity and cohesion in the whole. Axial lines may cross and recross one another, with their intersections possibly marked by some ornament. In the wilder parts these intersections can often be made interesting by treating them as clearings among trees, planted it may be with azaleas or lilies, or rhododendrons, or other plants that thrive in the half shade that would be given in such a position; or drifts of narcissi and bluebells could carpet the ground in spring. Axial lines should be given definite termination, and temples, arbours, garden ornaments, fountains, seats and wrought-iron gates may be placed to supply this interest. Again it must be understood that in this connection axial lines are not necessarily straight lines. . . .—*Modern Gardens*

BACKYARDS

There are many small town gardens that might aptly be described as backyards, with all the implications that such a description implies. Such spaces are often enclosed by buildings or walls and it might seem difficult to make them attractive. Space in London, and other cities is, however, aesthetically as well as financially valuable and such yards can with a little ingenuity and work often be transformed into delightful courts.—*The Creative Art of Garden Design*

BLUE BORDERS

Delphiniums in all shades of blue and purple are the glory of midsummer flower gardens. Their stately spires, planted at regular intervals down the length of a herbaceous border, give an idea of order that can be very satisfying and blue in its many tones goes happily with most other colours.—*The Creative Art of Garden Design*

CAMELLIAS

For what wonderful shrubs they are, evergreen, with light-reflecting foliage and producing in sheltered positions their exotic-looking flowers from the end of November until April.—*The Creative Art of Garden Design*

CLASSIFICATION

Gardens may be classified briefly into several kinds, according to the character of their design, their size, situation, the nature of their surroundings, etc. The smallest, which is generally the little garden of a town house, should be treated as a court of lawn or paving surrounded with flower filled borders. Then there is the larger town or suburban garden, generally of two or more divisions; it may be a lawn, herbaceous borders, a rose-garden, and perhaps a rock garden and glades, or a wild garden. There is also the larger town or smaller country garden, with lawns and often large trees and there are finally the more extensive grounds of country houses with formal gardens, lawns and trees, the whole possibly set in a park of smaller or greater extent. This last type may again be subdivided into two classes: one, the nicely balanced garden in which everything is newly planted and consciously kept to a certain scale; and secondly, and that generally the most extensive of all, in which spreading lawns and old timbered trees form the setting for the new formal gardens and informal glades.—*Modern Gardens*

CONSERVATISM

The making of a garden is the oldest of man's preoccupations and its history a tale of constant striving against difficulties. While progress and change have left their indelible mark upon this, one of the oldest of the arts, the conservative mind of many gardeners is still somewhat unreceptive to new ideas. Nor is this altogether a bad thing—as witness some of the atrocities that have been committed in other forms of art—and even in garden design itself.—*Garden Design,* Autumn 1938

COURTYARDS

A courtyard is defined by the Oxford dictionary as a space enclosed by walls or buildings. Courts may be large or small—size does not matter. They may be enriched with ornaments, not too many but showing real merit in their design and craftsmanship. Planting may be confined to climbing plants on the walls; there may be beds of shrubs or plants, or plants may be grown in pots or tubs, the latter chosen to form a decoration in themselves.—*The Creative Art of Garden Design*

DENMARK

There is a noticeably high standard of taste in Denmark both in architecture and the kindred arts, and here, as one would expect to find, gardens often exhibit a scholarly and refined treatment on broad lines.—*Modern Gardens*

DRAWING ROOMS

Formal, paved or sunk flower gardens may be described as the drawing-rooms of the garden, and should be furnished with the silks and tapestries of the flower world rather than with its cottons and chintzes. Begonias and salvias, choice lilies and gladioli, and even the rather too much despised geraniums, may all find a place here. There will also be heliotropes, carnations, and some of the wine red tobacco plants for their scent.—*Modern Gardens*

DRIVES AND FORECOURTS

Drives and forecourts are too often regarded as simply a means of approach to the house, but really the fact that the drive and forecourt constitute the introduction to both house and grounds is sufficient to call for the greatest care and attention in its planning and adornment. First impressions being so valuable, it is necessary to create an atmosphere, not only in accord with the style and property as a whole, but beautiful in itself . . .

The practical essentials in a forecourt are ease of approach and departure, space in which cars may turn comfortably and a smooth, firm, properly drained surface.—*Modern Gardens*

FRANCE

French gardens rely more upon a characteristic formality of planning and general design than upon effects of planting. Avenues of trees, fountains with their charm of outline, the formal placing of delightfully treated pavilions and gazebos—all these elements are woven into a unity, over which plays a charming fancy, typical of French art as a whole. Having fewer sources of interest than their English prototype on the horticultural side, they are an expression of the temperament of the nation, and a fitting accompaniment to the architecture they so suitably adorn. To institute a comparison—just as the masses of scarlet geraniums, which as a rule fill the beds surrounding the Victoria Memorial in front of Buckingham Palace, are probably the most suitable treatment with the architectural character of their surroundings, in the same way the patterned carpet bedding and formally placed statuary of the courts of the Louvre are entirely in harmony with Perault's lovely buildings. Versailles again, one of the best known examples of French gardens, is entirely French in its conception of formal planning. The proportions are perfect and each part contributes with well-judged harmony to the effect of the magnificently conceived whole. From the great terrace in front of the palace the vista, between woods, over lawns and water, is carried to the country beyond and to the distant horizon. The woods are intersected by lofty alleys, the open spaces decorated by fountains, each the work of an artist, yet all fitly expressing the thought of the master-mind of Le Nôtre, who planned the gardens in their entirety. The parterres are planted with the fine taste of the French, and, although much of the loveliness of the gardens has gone with the passing of the monarchy, their dignity remains untouched, and they are typical of the French love of symmetry and perfection of form.

This atmosphere of lightness and grace is equally characteristic of smaller French gardens with their rather formal treatment, judicious placing of statuary, pleasing use of fountains or pools, covered walks and arbours, and secondary use of plants. The quality of French gardens is typified by the lightness of wrought-iron balconies, so noticeable in French street architecture, as opposed to Italian stone balustrades, or English gardens of trees, lawns and flowers.—*Modern Gardens*

FRENCH RIVIERA

. . . there is sun and light and warmer days, often brilliant skies and that

The main lawn and formal borders at Hillside

Formal flower-garden once part of a kitchen-garden at Milton, near Peterborough

Gate opening into a walled flower-garden at Milton

The water garden at The Vern, Marden, Herefordshire

Formal flower-garden at The Vern

View from the formal flower-garden over the Clyde at Ardencraig, Isle of Bute

General view of the garden from the river at The Mill House, Fittleworth, Sussex

A wide paved terrace leading to lawns at The Mill House

clear air in which colour tells so vividly. But there is the mistral, that stormy wind from the north-west, which is bad for people and plants alike. Spring in such a climate is of course earlier and warmer, and because of this, gardens can be a wealth of colour when here trees and the earliest bulbs are opening. But while in warmer climates the quick rush to splendour is followed in midsummer by an arid dryness, in Britain a gradual development leads to all the brilliance of flowers and richness of foliage lasting well into the autumn.—*Garden Design,* Winter 1933

GERMANY AND AUSTRIA

. . . have many beautiful historical gardens, more especially those designed for their emperors and the numerous and powerful princes and reigning dukes, who vied with one another in the elaboration of their palaces and grounds. All of these show the marked characteristics of the Dutch, French and English schools as each in their turn became fashionable. During the sixteenth and seventeenth centuries Holland sent artists, craftsmen and garden makers to Germany, where they produced fine work in their own national style, and later in the eighteenth century the style of Le Nôtre was as prominent as in other parts of Europe. The actual work of this master is seen in the well-known gardens of the Palace of Herrenhausen in Germany and his influence in the Austrian gardens of Princes Liechtenstein and Schwartzenberg in Vienna. The next period dates from the end of the eighteenth century when English landscape gardening became the vogue, following much the same lines as it did in England and France.

German garden art of the nineteenth century bore the stamp of the 'Art Nouveau' style that swept Europe towards its close, and although traces of it remain it has been supplanted by . . . broader and more intelligible modern work . . .—*Modern Gardens*

GLADES

No part of the garden is easier to make and to maintain, nor can be lovelier, that a well-designed and carefully planted glade of trees and shrubs.

A glade may equally well be made on level or sloping ground but there must not be a straight line in its composition. It may be small or it may be extensive, but in every case its width should be proportional to its length.

Usually it consists of a lawn bordered with shrubs and trees so arranged that each shrub or tree can attain its own characteristic beauty of form and foliage, in addition to helping in the most effective way towards the ultimate beauty of the scene as a whole.—*Garden Design of Today*

Trees and turf are the foundations of natural beauty, and glades, in which natural beauty is heightened by art, can be some of the loveliest of garden scenes.—*The Studio,* July 1926

GOLDEN GARDENS

Sunlight streaming on to golden foliage, or on to yellow or golden flowers and foliage, can be opulent in its glowing colour. Gardens of gold or of gold and yellow need, and should be, in sun. Set in green foliage, so that one comes suddenly on to the surprise of it, such a garden could be as effective as it is easy to make and plant. Golden yews, the variety *Taxus baccata aurea,* should be planted to hedge it round, and it could be arranged in a set pattern of beds, with clipped golden yews planted symmetrically to emphasise the design. The beds could be filled with orange and yellow marigolds with coreopsis, nasturtium Golden Gleam, with yellow daisies, with soft yellow gaillardias, toning with, and adding to the brilliance of orange lilies, blazing in their golden setting.

. . . There should be a seat, . . . and there might be an old stone sundial in the middle. No other colours other than yellow and gold must be allowed to lessen its cheerful splendour. Such a garden would be at its best in the morning, with early sunlight flashing back in countless rays from the dew-covered flowers and petals. It would be worth leaving one's bed to see.—*Garden Design of Today*

GREEN

The tonal value of green is not always fully recognised. As an example, a walk of mown turf enclosed by hedges of cupressus or yew with perhaps a seat at each end and, if the walk is wide enough, cupressus or green or golden yews placed significantly down its length on both sides would be a welcome contrast to a rose garden or other gardens filled with colour . . .

Beware of having too much colour and an insufficient quantity of green. A garden containing no other colours than the varying shades of green, or with the addition of gold given by shrubs with golden variegations, may satisfy the most fastidious sense of beauty. Whilst one on which bright colours only are seen, with an insufficient or no green background, would fail to give pleasure; indeed in most people its glaring hues would arouse a feeling of positive aversion.—*My Garden, Illustrated,* April 1916

HOLLY

The glistening leaves . . . often so dark in themselves, reflect light to a surprising degree, so much so that their darkness seems lost in reflected sunlight.—*The Earth is my Canvas*

IRIS GARDENS

Irises . . . their grey-green, swordlike leaves look particularly well against flagstones and a paved iris garden can be a joy when the irises are flowering, and even later when their foliage is decorative.—*The Creative Art of Garden Design*

ITALY

Spouting columns of water rising to fall into basin after basin and then going one cannot see where, except that it is always rising, always to fall. Pools and running water splashing with rhythmic coolness in hot sun. Terraces and walls, and flights of stone or marble steps, with connecting walks between until the farthest garden is reached. Great pots and tubs of oleanders, crowning piers and walls and flanking steps; formal parterres filled with shrubs and flowers, marble loggias and statuary, singly, or grouped with that wealth of the sculptor's art, only to be seen in Italy. Cypress trees, darkly silhouetted against the clear southern sky. Thickets of ilex, their twisted stems crowned with dark foliage of olive green making densest shade beneath; heavy piers of pergolas, with light crossing of vine-covered treillage, giving needful shade, more beautiful here because more necessary than in cooler climes. Stone seats overlooking miles of *campagna* so extensive that in soft lights one can imagine it is the sea; or in the cities, tiled roofs with green and cypress trees amongst them, their widely overhanging eaves beautiful with strong light and shade as Italian roofs are. High walls and lower walks, and terraces, all perfectly formal and yet touched with the finger of age into softer beauty. With few flowers, but with rich foliage of cypress and ilex trees, completing as nothing else could the house for which it is the setting. Such are the traditional gardens of Italy, from which so much inspiration for formal work in other lands has been drawn.

Essentially Italian also are the smaller wall-enclosed courts overlooked by and giving light to the surrounding rooms. Again there would be one or more fountains placed centrally or against the walls, paving of brick, stone, or cobbles with flagged paths inset for pattern, and for comfort of walking. There would be stone benches or seats, and the walls, probably with rectangular panels slightly recessed, would be enriched with moulded coping, sculpture in low relief, niches and statues, perhaps a central fountain basin, oleander or other shrubs in tubs and vases, climbers on walls and treillage, and if the court is large enough, a few trees. Touch it with all the impress of age, and there is alike in small or larger court, a garden stamped with the strong and beautiful character of Italian art. But in their decay some gardens, particularly those of the summer villas of wealthy Romans, show how decadent Italian art in its later rococo periods became. Sculpture and ornaments with which the terraces and walks were overloaded was faulty as it was redundant. Limbs of cement have disappeared leaving the supporting rods onto which the artificial stone was modelled standing gauntly. Grotesques degenerated into absurdities, and fountains and waterworks were elaborated until dignity of planning was lost in bewildering intricacy of faulty detail. Arising partly from the fact that the wave of plant collecting had not then swept over the plant-loving world, and probably even more because, until the eighteenth century, a garden design had been almost entirely formal and that the weaving both of ground contours and plant masses into a synthetic and lovely unit, had never been practised, the older Italian gardens possessed to a peculiar degree the formal characteristics of Italian architecture. Their terraces were essentially a part of the house, and indeed the character of the palace (most of the historic gardens are the gardens of palaces) permeated the grounds to a marked degree. The far-reaching activities of the Renaissance had their influence on garden design as much as on architecture, sculpture, painting, and artistic life generally. This was particularly the case in Italy, where the architecture of the palace and its garden setting of terraces were so intimately related.—*Modern Gardens*

JAPAN

Art to the Japanese is part of life, their objects of every day use are beautiful, and their beautiful things are useful and full of meaning. Japanese gardens are almost entirely landscape in character, formalism as it is understood in Europe and America scarcely entering into their design. The balanced massing of trees and plants, the placing of each separate unit in the general scheme and the resultant beauty of proportion of the garden as a whole are their essential qualities. To the Japanese a garden is full of symbolism, of meaning in the use of the materials of which it is composed. Every Japanese garden is essentially a composition, the picture being built up to a central point of interest, and coarseness weeded out by a subtle finesse of selection until its beauty steals into the senses to remain there as an enduring delight. In the days of old Japan, before Western commercialism had penetrated into the life of the country, every common thing expressed a divinity. A god guarded every utensil or tool, and spoke from every stone and tree. A man entered his garden, and his cares were left behind, the spirit of peace was there, palpably present, and making it to the receptive temperament of the Japanese a place of blessing and repose, a place wherein his mind went towards another world. But in all their simplicity, these beautiful gardens are made, their stones are brought to them, often from long distances, and trees are trained into their perfection of form and scale by unremitting care and patience. Some of the larger stones, too big to move, are carefully broken into sections, their separate parts numbered, and after removal they are pieced together and joined with an invisible cement. These stones, which are sometimes so large and always so carefully placed that they give the impression of belonging naturally to the garden, often form the chief interest around which the composition is built. The same care is used in the choice and planting of trees, which are treasured in proportion to the time and trouble spent on their training. Years of careful tending and pruning go to their making, coniferous and deciduous alike; they are transplanted at any age, and have at the same time every appearance of having grown and developed naturally in their new quarters. This is the case with everything in a Japanese garden. The stones of rocky water channels show the same care and attention to the smallest detail, even to the placing of large clumps of growing moss between them and on the ground around tree roots.

The use of trees and plants, too, that have completed their allotted growth enables the garden designer to obtain perfection of balance as he works, without, as in other countries, having to wait for it to develop, and without risk of its being spoiled by irregularities of growth. Proportion is the root of all successful design, and this is the case to an even greater degree with landscape than with formal gardens. It is partly owing to this, and to the fact that their garden scenery is so skilfully related to the distant landscape, that the small Japanese garden appears so much larger than it really is. . . .

There is, in Japan, a superstition, carefully observed, that water must follow the course of the sun, and no matter what extra trouble may be involved, it is invariably arranged that any stream should enter from the east and flow in a westerly direction. . . .

It was during the Ashikaga Regents, in the fifteenth century, that two typically Japanese arts, Tea Ceremonial and Flower Arrangement, which have had a very considerable influence on Japanese gardening, first became popular. As the rite of tea drinking became more ceremonial, the one or perhaps two garden rooms dedicated to this purpose and the garden surrounding them were given more particular attention, until they became the most beautiful parts of the grounds. It was from this time that gardens were designed to be in harmony with the architectural character of the buildings in them, but although some were formally treated those surrounding the Cha-no-yu ('Tea Ceremony') were still kept entirely informal in the traditional Japanese manner.

One naturally associates a Japanese garden with almond blossom and flower-laden plum and cherry trees, with wistaria and acacias and Japanese maples, with iris and much colour generally—and rightly so at certain seasons of the year. The Japanese, however, have long appreciated the fact that balance and proportion create a deeper and more subtle beauty than do masses of colour, and these gardens are often for considerable periods places of green trees and plants, and beautifully placed stones and water. The traditional Japanese garden is a scene of quiet beauty in which life's cares may be forgotten. Its owner knows the loveliness of a single almond or cherry tree with flower wreathed boughs, telling against the darker background of fir or other trees; the soft shades of iris and wistaria and all the richness of varied shades of green, from tones that are almost gold to others that are nearly black.—*Modern Gardens*

JUNE

June is here, royal in loveliness, the season of crowding blossoms, crushed and dewy scents, the last strains of the nightingale's song: the English June, with which no other can compare. People who have travelled in wide and brilliant lands where sunshine (and dust) can be counted on for three unbroken months, declare that all England is a garden, green and fragrant. We can afford to look about us complacently, at the hedgerows—the garden of the wayfarer—at cottage plots half buried in lush valleys, at the gardens enfolded in the verdure of vast parks, and agree that what our admirers say is true. In a reserved island fashion we take pride in our own share of it. We remember the lashings we have endured, the cold and cheerless days, the banked fogs that have conspired together to create the bewildering beauty of the English June.

It is a curiously blended beauty, sensuous and spiritual, wherein the delight of the eyes has but a share. The feeling of physical well-being, the effect of sunshine's caresses, the sudden realising of sensations which November had laid dismally to rest with candle, book and bell, are all tangled up in our frank adoration of summer. Under the spell of June we have fallen in love with life again.—*Garden Design,* Summer 1936

LANDSCAPE GARDENING

... as a term is of too wide application. It implies the opposite of formal design, and should signify the creating of effects by studied management of the soil and by informal arrangements of trees, plants and lawns. In a purely landscape garden there would be no walls, paved paths, or formal pools, only the natural effects produced by beautiful contours of the ground, with planting of trees, shrubs and flowers all arranged with the nicest regard to rhythm of line, and balance of form and colour. There might be natural water but no formal pools, rock and wild but no formal gardens, stepping stones but no formal paths.—*Modern Gardens*

LIFE

Life has a wonderful way of compensating and balancing. The fewer one has of those pleasures that make the strongest personal appeal, the greater the enjoyment of that limited amount of pleasure, and possibly no people enjoy so fully the delights of gardens and of the country as those who have perforce lived gardenless in towns. To look from one's windows on to turf and trees, instead of on to bricks and mortar. To go from one's own door on to one's own lawn, to watch the first buds break and the first shoots appear in one's own garden is a much more intense and intimate pleasure than it is to see it in some public park, and, again the law of compensation, it is winter makes the high enjoyment of summer just as, if time were one long, continuing summer, we should get tired of it, and long for winter.—*Garden Design*, Winter 1933

LIGHT

Very much depends on light (for flowers in herbaceous borders). In midsummer, with its strong sunshine and clear air, colour grouping should be carefully arranged so that, however brilliant, the strongest of varying colours, when seen together, are harmonious. In autumn with its softer skies and lower tones of light, there is less need for this care, and colours that together would be discordant in summer, please. As well as the softer lights there is some harmonising quality of tone in autumn flowers and foliage—rich and beautiful in their mixture of many colours.—*Garden Design of Today*

MAGNOLIAS

. . . are so decorative both in their waxen flowers and in the almost architectural quality of their handsome foliage that they should find a place in all gardens that are not too cold or exposed.—*The Earth is my Canvas*

PERGOLAS

. . . are shaded ways, green cloisters of shadow, colour and perfume. In midsummer, when the heat rises in waves from sun-scorched turf, it is agreeable to sit or stroll within such green and pleasant walks, under vines and roses, honeysuckle, jessamines, and other beautiful and fragrant climbers.—*Garden Design of Today*

The formality of the gardens is accentuated by their contrast with the curving lines of the glades at Bowhill in Sussex

Steps leading to the main lawn at Bowhill

The south terrace and formal gardens at Lower Sandhill, Halland, Sussex

The enclosed garden gives a feeling of seclusion yet spaciousness at The Old Forge, Henley-on-Thames, Oxfordshire

A formal garden enclosed by red brick walls at *The White House, Highgate, London*

A paved court with a stone bench and a variety of pots and other containers at *The White House*

A sunken garden gives protection to the plants at The White House, Sandwich

The lower terrace with roses, delphiniums, and nepeta at Ardleigh, Chigwell, Essex

PLAN

A plan is an aerial view of the plot taken from an impossible height, so that ordinary perspective really becomes cartography. Such a plan is an essential preliminary if the plotting is to be made into a coherent scheme, as it shows at a glance the relation of one part to another, and it is interesting to note that a plan which looks a well-balanced composition on paper usually satisfies when it is translated into actual fact.

It is difficult for many people to visualise the finished result from a plan only, and plans by themselves can be misleading, even to those accustomed to reading them. An architect's drawing for a house conveys a clear picture of the finished product—but how can one do justice to the lovely and inconstant forms and colouring of nature, by means of a paper presentation only? It is of course an impossibility.—*Garden Design,* Summer 1937

PURPOSE

The main purpose of a private garden is to provide a suitable and beautiful setting for the house which is its *raison d'être.* Gardens, if they are to be beautiful, must, whether large or small, have certain qualities. They should be planned on proportionately broad and generous lines and they must have good proportions in their separate parts. They must be happily related to their surroundings, and the trees, shrubs and plants with which they are furnished must be arranged with due regard to balance and contrast of form.—*The Earth is my Canvas*

RELATIONSHIP

The close relationship between house and gardens is all-important and cannot be over-stressed; the two should relate so easily and naturally, that each may seem the essential complement of the other. Nearly every site has an atmosphere peculiarly its own, and the garden designer is successful in so far as he realises this principle and works in accordance with its dictates.—*Modern Gardens*

ROCK-GARDENS

To introduce in miniature, something of the effects of mountain scenery, and to combine with it the most beautiful plants available, is to add a constant and varied source of interest to the garden. . . . Even a small rock-garden may, by artistry of arrangement in the placing of stone and the massing and composition of colour, be touched into wonderful beauty. The contours of the land will sometimes suggest the site; a natural hollow most readily lends itself to rock formation; but this is by no means essential, as by the removal of soil to a slight depth and by using the soil so removed to form the surrounding banks, the necessary formation is effected.

There is risk of the small rock-garden degenerating into the 'rockery.' The one can be beautiful, the other is generally a heap or heaps of stone-dotted soil without line or proportion. At its smallest a rock garden should be a sunk path between stones, with planting on either side, but there must be the two sides, not a single bank. Each stone should be placed to give a definite feeling of line and rhythm, and this result is obtained more effectively by using a comparatively small number of large, rather than a greater number of small stones. If this value of line is absent the garden must lack that complete charm and beauty that can only result from the perfect disposition of stones and plants, with perhaps the addition of turf and water.—*Modern Gardens*

ROSE-GARDEN

The intimacy and privacy of an enclosed space—the restful symmetry of ordered beds, enriched by the many colours to be found in the roses of today—is as much a necessity in a garden scheme as is the study or library in the house. . . . The spirit of peace and harmony which should pervade the formal rose-garden comes of good design and conscious planning, and not of a haphazard collection of beds planted indiscriminately, or of commonplace ornament. The flowering periods of each variety, arrangement of colour and habit of growth, are some of the more important considerations. The design of the enclosure should be determined by the character of the site and by the general lay-out of the whole garden scheme . . . it should be based, in general, on some geometrical plan, such as a circle, an octagon or a square . . . the beds should not be too large in proportion and yet each should give an effective mass of colour. The centre of the garden may be emphasised by a figure in lead or stone, an old well-head or a sun-dial, and, since the garden is filled with colour and scent and the charm which comes from the blending of these two, a seat recess, in the enclosing hedge on the centre line of a main pathway, should not be omitted.—*Garden Design of Today*

SHADOW

The blindest among us know that a lawn is only brilliantly green when the skies are grey, that the sun is indeed a colossal thief. But to have our eyes thoroughly opened we should study a garden where the shadows of trees fall across a stretch of lawn, a deep flower border and a stone path. The lawn shadow is deep green, that on the flowers is gloriously muddled grey-ruby and lapis lazuli, that on the stone pure cobalt blue.—*Garden Design, Summer 1936*

SHRUBBERY

. . . that loathsome word, reminiscent of green laurel, aucubas, golden privet, and an occasional overgrown lilac.—*Garden Design of Today*

SITES

Probably those are easiest to treat in which the residence stands on a slight eminence with a gradual fall from the garden front, which preferably faces south or south-west. Such sites could be easily and effectively treated as terraced gardens having walls or banks, and steps separating and connecting the different levels. Steps should be wide and shallow, and where there is a succession of stairways on an axial line, the levels and steps should (if the lie of the ground permits) be so arranged that the whole length of the vista can be seen from either end. Comparatively level or slightly undulating sites, again, are as a rule easy to treat, and with properly proportioned masses of planting may be made to appear larger than can a hillside garden, and can be given a quiet beauty, of a character entirely different to that of terraces and walls.

Perhaps the most difficult are those in which the ground rises from the terrace in front of the house, when unless the levels be carefully treated, the house will always have an unpleasantly sunk appearance. . . .

In the case of sites on which the position of the house has to be chosen, its orientation would naturally be such that the garden front and reception rooms face as near south as possible. If there is a choice of levels it should generally be built on the higher ground.—*Modern Gardens*

SMALL GARDENS

By a sense of right feeling, and care in planning, it is possible to have very charming scenes in the smallest of gardens. Nothing of undue size or importance must be allowed. The resultant effects must display everywhere evidence of the nicest sense of proportion and fitness in every arrangement, and it will be seen that, although greater grandeur may be created by extent of ground and elaborate and costly work, yet very charming and lovely scenes may be obtained without any great outlay or pretentious schemes either in cost or detail.—*My Garden, Illustrated,* April 1916

SPRING

Spring fever, that most pleasant and demoralising of ailments, is going its rounds, leaving the patient liable to get up at any moment and go out and start poking about, digging and weeding; nothing so rapturous as the first bout of weeding, nothing so dreary, stale and unprofitable as the fifty-first. The odd thing is that it is always the first. *On revient toujours à ses premiers amours.* No other spring has ever been but this; no other birds piped on the bough, no other green sunset light turned the world into so completely magic a place. . . .

The time has come when 'garden' is a word in everybody's mouth. Gardens have become real places again, peeped at first thing in a morning and last thing at night.—*Garden Design,* Spring 1937

SWEDEN

During the time of their widespread activities a number of fine schemes were carried out in Sweden in which the influence of Le Nôtre is predominant. Apart from this no gardens of outstanding importance have been made until comparatively recent times. The most characteristic expression of Swedish architecture is seen in their castles, whose walls enclose finely-treated courtyards of an entirely formal nature. They are picturesque in themselves, and generally blend in the happiest way with romantic settings of hills and lakes or sea.—*Modern Gardens*

TERRACES

One of our most delightful memories of Italy and the French Riviera is that of terraced gardens on sunny hillsides. They marked for us a high note of the beauty and glamour of the South. Marble stairways broken by level gardens descended, one could imagine, straight into sea or lake, their gleaming paleness accented by dusky-green of cypresses standing singly, like sentinels, or ranked like colonnades, on the slopes.

We remember many a glittering hillside villa where summer seemed to have stood still; how delightful to live in such an eyrie, looking down on a garden so banked on the slopes that although it lay spread at one's feet, it still could keep its secrets! We came back and said that nothing in England could compare with those stabs of colour, those dark shafts of trees, those generous stairways and courts in which the sun made a dial of its own.

It does not always occur to us that this treatment of a hillside is partly derived from centuries-old tradition which insisted, in a garden, on the severest formality on very sharp perpendicular and horizontal accents; partly on the strong sunlight which makes for wealth in sculptured form rather than colour; partly on the gardener's instinct to enrich and strengthen that which Nature has offered him.

In point of fact there are hundreds of sites in English hilly counties where most effective gardens could be made. Take the scarp slope of the Chilterns, for example, where in many places the hillside drops like a table cloth. The difficulty is that although we are the greatest garden lovers in Europe, we have not the structural instinct. Our tendency has always been to plant a few roots and hope for the best; if our gardens happen on a slope—well it might be easier to get up and down in wet weather if we made a few steps.

It is not necessary for a sloping garden to be Italianate to be beautiful, but we might keep in our memory as a challenge, those gardens which are first a piece of architecture and then a place where flowers grow. We might also remember that the Latin people envy us our soft lights, our restful limpid greenery as much as we envy them their ultramarine seas and skies, their statuesque forms. With a little forethought and definite planning it should not be impossible to unite some of their graces with our own.—*Garden Design,* Autumn 1936

TOPIARY

Topiary or clipped shrubs suitably placed will give a charming age-old flavour to a formal walk or garden, or again a topiary garden made of little else than clipped shrubs, hedges and lawn can be delightful.

Because they are slow and dense in their habit of growth, yew and box are the two most suitable shrubs for cutting into the curious shapes that are the essence of topiary work. Birds, animals, fish, or the quaint pyramidal forms that were so characteristic a feature in the Elizabethan garden can all be used with the most pleasing results.

It is an interesting task to use one's ingenuity in forming the various topiary pieces, but it is a task requiring some skill and experience in its performance, and it is usually advisable to buy them ready grown. Topiary has two principal values. One, its endless possible variety of form; the other, the light and shade which these forms give. Moreover, green in its many tones is an extraordinary valuable colour. In sunshine it glistens in countless facets of reflected light, while in shadow its sombre darkness is almost black. Topiary is equally effective standing against bright green turf or silhouetted clear cut against blue sky.—*Garden Design of Today*

VICTORIAN GARDENS

It is astonishing to see how almost every canon of good taste seemed to be ignored in many Victorian gardens. There was, judged by the standards of today, little, if any, regard for line and mass, balance and proportion, and there was seldom cohesion in the relation of their various parts; the particular character or atmosphere of the place was seldom taken into account, and there was little, if any attempt to effectively develop existing features of interest. Gravel walks intersected lawns, which were further cut up with beds of all sizes and shapes, filled with bedding plants crude in colour and generally without interest, or beauty of form and colour. Victorian gardens also show in their planting little evidence of the lovely groupings of colour that can be arranged with the endless number of plants at the garden maker's use. Perhaps this is not to be wondered at from people who could wear or tolerate such absurdities in dress as bustles and crinolines.—*Garden Design,* Spring 1935

WATER

Winding through trees, tumbling over grey rocks, and winding into sunlit or dark still pools, running water will, by its freshness, its shadowy depths, and the intricacy and strangeness of its reflections, add more to the enchantment of a garden scheme than many more pretentious features.—*Garden Design of Today*

WHITE GARDENS

One scarcely realises how many shades of white there are until one comes to use them.—*The Creative Art of Garden Design*

WINTER

The real English winter is a beautiful spectacle of low-keyed tones, of tender colour ranges never seen in summer, of horizons widening and contours changing because of the absence of leaves, of incredibly lovely skies where stars wink at you through branches whose bare lives are enchanting enough to make one hate summer for evermore. To appreciate this presupposes a good physical state and complete indifference to climatic conditions. Probably the only people who really love winter are those who ride or hunt, and vagrant poets and painters who delight in the spectacle of the naked trees, the glimmering vale, the iridescent surface lights on plough and pasture, the blue of the rain-washed, pale sky, the delicious smell of the sodden paths in the woods.

But these vagrants for the most part do not possess gardens; and perhaps they live in the shadow of those who do. A garden lover looks at winter from still another angle. Winter is the alternate bully and fondler who throttles out of existence or persuades to smile too soon his dearest plants.—*Garden Design,* Winter 1936

A stream falls from pool to pool at Long View, Reigate Heath, Surrey

Appendix
A Selection of Cane Gardens

LONDON

Bow, E.3. Bryant & Mays.
Courtyard at the factory and alterations and decorations to directors' dining room and offices.

2 Catherine Street, S.W.1. Sir Austin Harris, K.B.E.
Roof garden with surrounding pergola.

Fleet Street, E.C.4. Hoare's Bank.
With its stone-curbed pool and its flower-filled stone boxes this inner court, which dates back to 1829, is an unexpected oasis among the bricks and mortar of Fleet Street.

115 Frognal, N.W.3. S. M. Duncan.
A small formal garden enclosed by brick walls and buildings in character with the pleasant Georgian house.

Ivy House, North End, Hampstead. Anna Pavlova.
Stone balconies were added to the house. The conservatory was converted into an aviary for sub-tropical birds. In the lowest part of the garden was a pool with swans, reminiscent of the Swan Lake ballet.

King George's Park, Wandsworth.
As well as providing sports facilities, it is designed as a stretch of country scenery in one of London's very built-up areas. A long, curving centre glade is enclosed on both sides by conifers and flowering trees and shrubs and off the centre glade, each in its own decorative setting, are the various facilities for sport and games.

Spedan Tower, West Heath Road, Hampstead, N.W.3. B. Brenninkmeyer.
A garden in which London and the country met. Beautiful skylines, modelled by magnificent trees. Pool garden, tennis courts, rock garden, glades.

The White House, Highgate. Mr. and Mrs. Clifford Curzon.
The terrace is formal; the central glade lawn is informal. The pool-garden to which the long glade leads is entirely formal while two gardens on the southern side of the house are again formal but with quite a different character. Together they make a set of gardens, each contrasting with the others, but all harmoniously welded into one. The loggia was added as a kind of open-air dining-room.

Witanhurst, Highgate. Sir Arthur and Lady Crosfield.
A formal garden enclosed by red-brick walls at least a century or two old,

against which the colour of its flowers takes on an added value. From the tower wall there is a wonderful view with Ken Wood in the distance. A summer house or garden pavilion built in a corner formed by the higher walls is fitted with electric lighting, heating and telephone.

BEDFORDSHIRE

Hatley Park, Sandy. Herman Lebus.
Long terrace and extensive gardens and glades with lake and mature trees.

Westfields, Oakley, Bedford. E. F. Davison.
Approached by a long drive it is in a pleasantly secluded position more or less in the centre of its own timbered meadows. The garden includes formal and informal water-gardens, rose-garden, glades of trees and shrubs and herbaceous and other borders.

Woburn Abbey. The Duke of Bedford.
The pleasure grounds and the park were laid out to designs by Humphrey Repton. Now a formal garden and glades with flowering trees and shrubs by Cane give additional interest to the pleasure grounds.

BERKSHIRE

Bodens Ride, Swinley Forest, Ascot. Sir Edward Peacock.
Terrace, summerhouse, pergola, glade and wild garden.

Charters, Sunninghill, Ascot. Sir Charles and Lady Shaw.
Terraces, glades, lawns and drive.

Kingswood House, Sunningdale, Ascot. Sir Herbert Samuelson.
Terrace, pergola, water-garden and rhododendron glades.

Little Bowden, Pangbourne. Captain and Mrs. Tudor Crosthwaite.
Complete design, lawns, glade, herbaceous borders.

West Woodhay House, Newbury. Harry Henderson, Trustees of West Woodhay Estate.
A drive between magnificent trees, formal garden and bridge to a glade on far side of lake.

Woodhay, Sunningdale. Captain and Mrs. Leslie J. Taylor.
Rhododendron and other glades, herbaceous borders, all in a setting of old trees.

BUCKINGHAMSHIRE

Germains, Chesham. Walter M. N. Reid.
Paved garden, topiary work. Massive clipped box.

The Old Parsonage, Marlow. Colonel and Mrs. Orr.
Although comparatively small this garden has a charm that comes partly from the tiled roofs and gables of nearby buildings. It has the formality of a garden enclosed within its own boundary walls.

*The stone-curbed pool and flower-filled stone containers in the courtyard of
Hoare's Bank, Fleet Street, London*

CAMBRIDGESHIRE

Milton, Peterborough. The Earl Fitzwilliam.
 With part of it dating back to the sixteenth century Milton is architecturally one of the finest houses in the country. The park was laid out by
 Repton. Formerly part of a kitchen-garden with formal flower-garden
 surrounded by high brick walls and yew hedges, this garden is full of
 colour and fragrance.

DEVON

Dartington Hall, Totnes. Mr. and Mrs. Leonard Elmhirst.
 The development of these lovely gardens has been going on since 1927.
 Cane took over the planning in 1945. He cut through the thick, wild,
 overgrown upper areas to open up vistas and create special features of
 interest. He created the glade and the flight of steps leading from it down
 to the lower end of the tournament ground. He also cleared High
 Meadow and made of it a pleasant, peaceful upper region of the garden
 with a new vista to the Hall. Other parts of the gardens were also
 cleared under his direction and simplified, and his work includes the new
 entrance drive, the remaking of the upper road and the planning of the
 azalea dell.

ESSEX

Ardchoille, Frinton-on-Sea. Major MacGregor McGrigor.
 The gardens have a continuance of formal design which extends from the
 terrace down the steps into the rose-garden; this is in marked contrast to
 the surrounding lawn, glades, borders and herbaceous walk.

Ardleigh, Chigwell. S. J. Ercolani.
 The ground slopes steeply down from the principal garden front to the
 southern boundary, and on the steep gradient walls are built to support
 the terrace. There are an upper and lower terrace, a rose walk, a glade
 and a little stream in which water falls via several rockbound pools.

1 Broomhill Walk, Woodford. Dr. A. A. Hoda.
 Though the garden is small, the rhythmic treatment of softly curving
 steps and borders creates an illusion of greater size than would have been
 given by a more formal treatment.

The Cottage, Felsted. Edwin Trow.
 A miniature paved garden where the walls and a projecting wing of the
 house enclose a small court, recessed on one side and surrounded by
 borders of old-fashioned flowers.

Glengarry, Stanway. Miss Wagstaff.
 A simply designed small garden with lawn, flower and shrub borders,
 rock- and rose-garden and a little paved court.

The Hall, Tendring. S. V. D. Douglas-Jones.
 Formal pool-garden and rhododendron glade leading to and continuing
 round a lake are the main features.

An oasis among bricks and mortar. Courtyard at Hoare's Bank

A pool in the glade enclosed by Scots pines at Westwoods, Windlesham, Surrey

A paved path leading to the lower lawns and lake at Westwoods

Formal gardens blending into a parklike setting of pastures and trees at Busbridge Wood, Godalming, Surrey

The Howe, Halstead.
Rose-garden with paved walk, glade and rock-garden.

Langham Hall, Colchester. Colonel Maturin-Baird.
On a level plateau which overlooks the valley of the River Stour, Langham Hall is in Constable country and a walk leading to a pool in the grounds is the subject of one of his paintings. There is a painting of Langham Church in the Tate Gallery.

Lea Rigg, Brentwood. Stamp W. Wortley.
A paved terrace, lawns, tennis-court, a small formal garden and informal glades and natural gardens.

The Long House, Frinton-on-Sea. Lowther Kemp.
A terrace, rose-garden, herbaceous border, glade and groups of willows and birches.

The Middlesex Hospital Convalescent Home, Clacton.
Formerly the kitchen-garden. With its seats and shelters, its spacious lawns, long straight borders in front of the building and its extensive glade leading to an enclosed formal garden. the grounds fulfil their purpose and provide a scene of peace and seclusion for patients and staff in a setting rich with the colours and fragrance of flowers and foliage.

The Mill House, Felsted. Mrs. Fletcher.
A southern aspect is backed by red brick walls and tiled roofs. French windows open on to a paved terrace. The ground falls away quite sharply and steps formed of blocks of stone give access to gardens on the lower level.

Old Hall Cottage, Frinton-on-Sea. W. Lowther-Kemp.
A small garden made to appear as large as possible by the skilful use of curving lines and by keeping everything to scale.

HAMPSHIRE

Headbourn Worthy, Nr. Winchester. Bernard Martin.
Old-fashioned garden with tennis-court, paved pergola made of larch poles, stepped to agree with contours, herbaceous borders and lawns.

West Meon House, Nr. Petersfield. L. D. Stent.
Formerly a bishop's palace. The gardens are an appropriate and pleasant setting for the dignified elevations of the house.

HEREFORDSHIRE

The Vern, Marden. R. S. de Quincey.
Views of the River Lugg with Dinmore Hill rising steeply, and beautifully wooded, on the far side. The outer garden is a simple prelude to the inner formal gardens in which the different heights and levels of the walls give the opportunity for an unusually effective treatment.

HERTFORDSHIRE

Bricket Wood. Lady Yule.
Terraces, informal water-garden with bridge, and lawns with borders of shrubs and flowering plants.

KENT

Greenways, Walmer. Mrs. Peek.
On the entrance front a formal treatment for the length of the site; a sunken pool-garden, a rose-garden and glades surround the house at Greenways.

The Kent Oil Refinery, Isle of Grain. Anglo-Iranian Oil Company.
Although in the strict sense of the word there are no gardens, the lawns, their surfaces chequered by the shade of trees, make with the enclosing hedges and shelter planting a dignified and suitable setting for these exposed offices and laboratory buildings.

The White House, Sandwich Bay. R. G. Chittenden.
Nothing between the garden and the sea but a stretch of sandy foreshore. A sunken garden gives protection to the plants. And, too, on the north side the curve of the low swelling hills give additional protection.

MIDDLESEX

The Aviary, Southall, Whitney and Lady Daphne Straight.
Occupies a site on what was formerly part of Osterley Park. Has a collection of rare birds. The gardens, lake and woodlands combine to make varied pleasure grounds and scenery as a setting for a house only half an hour's motor ride from the centre of London.

Old Meadows, West Drayton. Miss Emilie Grigsby.
Shows the value of a quadrangle of lawn as a setting for a country cottage.

OXFORDSHIRE

The Old Foundry, Henley-on-Thames. W. Sedgwick Rough.
The small, enclosed garden with its background of conifers and flowering shrubs gives a feeling of complete seclusion and, because it is level, of comparative spaciousness.

SURREY

Alderbrook Park, Cranleigh. Albert Van den Bergh.
Formal terraces and extensive wild gardens making a set of interesting and beautiful gardens, against their setting of tree and heather covered hills. Loggia, stairway, rose-garden, lawns, borders, walks, statuary.

Busbridge Wood, Godalming. J. E. Ferguson.
A long, straight herbaceous walk, a formal paved rose-garden, an azalea walk leading into a garden of flowering trees and shrubs, and a

rhododendron glade make a set of gardens varied in their separate parts and merging harmoniously into their park-like setting of pastures and trees.

Foxhills, Chertsey. The Hon. James and Mrs. A. Borthwick.
A water-garden which forms the termination of a long herbaceous walk is enclosed by yew hedges in a setting of old forest trees.

Green Glade, Wentworth. C. W. J. Tennant.
Broad walk, lawns and borders, informal pools and rills, fountain court and terrace.

Hascombe Court, Godalming. Sir John Jarvis.
A series of formal terraces, gardens and lawns on the higher level, enclosed by woodland walks and wild gardens into which Brenda's Walk, so called after one of Sir John's daughters, and a far terrace extend.

The King's House Garden, Burhill. H.M. Queen Elizabeth.
Garden for a house which was to have been presented by the Royal Warrant Holders Association to King George V on the occasion of his Jubilee. In its setting of old beeches and oaks, with light foliage of silver birches and with its views of the fairways on the golf-course, the house and gardens make an entity and give an impression of having been in existence for a long time.

Little Paddocks, Sunninghill. Lieut.-Col. J. N. Horlick.
Large rose-garden; flower walk bounded on one side by a high yew hedge while on the other merging into a background of decorative shrubs. The central flagged path has borders of carefully arranged colours, and there is a pool and a raised fountain basin.

Long View, Reigate Heath.
A design for a garden rising from the house. Wide, shallow steps rise from the terrace to the glade which again rises to a seat at the far end, the highest part of the garden. On one side a stream falling from pool to pool, and on the other a paved walk with steps made necessary by the rising ground together make for an interesting and beautiful garden.

Park Place, Egham. The Hon. Mrs. F. W. Maude.
Rose-garden, pergola and glades with the forecourt not separate from the garden.

Pixholme Court, Dorking. Sir J. Malcolm Fraser, Bart.
The gardens take advantage of the beauty of the wooded slopes of Box Hill. A 'golden' garden has a figure of Diana by Alfred J. Oakley.

St. Anne's Hill, Chertsey. Sir Gomer Berry.
The hill is treated as a beauty spot. There are glades cut through the forest trees with seats overlooking the valley beneath with its silvery stretches of the River Thames.

Westwoods, Windlesham. Arthur Pyke.
The gardens are enclosed by belts of Scots pines and tall rhododendrons. The aim in remaking was to heighten as much as possible the natural beauties of the site. Streams in the upper garden discharge their waters into a small lake near the lower boundary.

Windlesham Park. The Hon. and Mrs. Alec Henderson.
Herbaceous borders and water-garden. The forecourt was lowered to give the effect of raising the architecturally very pleasing house and a dry paved walk was laid all the way round the gardens.

Windycroft, near Godalming. C. A. Stedall.
House designed by Sir Henry Tanner. Grounds treated in such a way as to give shelter, colour, formality and wildness all within the limits of three acres.

SUSSEX

Bowhill, near Chichester. Mrs. M. L. MacDougall.
Straight lines and massed colours of a herbaceous walk are an important part of the design as a whole; the formality of the formal gardens is accentuated by their contrast with the curving lines of the glades.

Chestham Park, Henfield. Prince Littler, C.B.E.
Broad walks and formal gardens contrast with extensive glades of flowering trees and shrubs. Water-garden and large rose-garden.

Lower Sandhill, Halland, Lewes. Mrs. Kirwan-Taylor.
Shows what can be done to adapt existing features to other uses. A swimming-pool has been constructed in what was a small farmyard in which an existing barn was converted into a pavilion and dressing rooms. A formal walk extends along the length of the gardens.

The Mill House, Fittleworth. Brigadier G. P. Hardy-Roberts, C.B., C.B.E.
Built of stone and mellowed brick. An old mill still stands in the gardens to which the river, pools and stone walls give an unusual character.

Pilgrim's Cottage, Itchenor. Leslie D. Goldsmith.
The house with white walls and thatched roof stands near the southern boundary and the drive passing the entrance front goes on to a courtyard which is itself an attractive part of the gardens. An outstanding feature is the central glade, leading into a long walk on the eastern and a rose-garden on the western sides.

Sharnden, Mayfield. Mr. and Mrs. Sam Dennis.
House and terrace stand on high ground overlooking park-like scenery. In order to keep the natural beauty unspoiled and starting from the terrace a paved walk leads to extensive gardens which were made well to the east. Here from a long terrace several flights of steps at intervals descend to formal gardens. The whole scheme is surrounded by a spacious glade of flowering trees and shrubs.

WARWICKSHIRE

Bankside, Four Oaks, Sutton Coldfield. F. C. Hammond.
A continuous sweep of lawn, a formal paved terrace and rose-garden, a glade of flowering trees and shrubs, flower borders, an orchard and a small rock- and water-garden. all planned to give the feeling of greatest space and continuity in the one area.

Broadgate Garden, Coventry.
Given by the Dutch as a mark of their appreciation of the hospitality of the English people to Queen Wilhelmina during the war. It forms a setting for Sir William Reid Dick's statue of Lady Godiva.

Hillside, Four Oaks. Mrs. Whitworth.
Enclosed on three sides by mature forest trees, Hillside, although in a residential area, has the privacy of a country garden.

Sandy Bank, Sutton Coldfield.
Treatment for the gardens which were made on ground rising rather steeply from the house and terrace: there is a formal rose terrace between the house and the lawn; there are, too, a stream-garden and a paved herbaceous walk with steps made necessary by the rising ground.

Stoneleigh Abbey, Kenilworth. Lord and Lady Leigh.
A terraced setting for one of England's old and stately homes. The formality of the symmetrically arranged beds filled with scarlet geraniums with dark Irish yews gives a setting best suited to the dignified architecture of the Palladian façade.

Woodmead, Four Oaks, Sutton Coldfield. J. Whitworth.
The paved terrace and the lawn onto which the house opens give space and distance, while the comparatively small garden has the variety and interest of a paved herbaceous walk, a little separate rose-garden, a pool-garden and a rhododendron glade.

WILTSHIRE

Hungerdown House, Seagry, Near Chippenham. Egbert C. Barnes.
The site occupies a sloping shelf overlooking the upper valley of the Bristol Avon. In order that the house should not give the appearance of being perched rather insecurely on this slope, steps, walls and so on were used to give a sense of stability and formality.

WORCESTERSHIRE

The Avoncroft Museum of Buildings, Stoke Prior, Bromsgrove.
An unusual feature, the model village was inaugurated by Mr. L. G. Harris and aims to collect various buildings and industries from a wide radius and rebuild them in as attractive and suitably related a setting as possible. To do this is necessarily a work of some time.

YORKSHIRE

Nawton Tower, York. Lord Feversham.
A long terrace with continuous steps descending to a lower lawn. Wide walks lead through beds of drifts of heather, shrubs and roses to a lovely glade at the far end of the gardens.

Stonely Woods, Fadmoor, York. Sir Charles Richmond Brown.
The house opens onto a spacious terrace. This terrace is sheltered on

both ends by high stone walls. In front to the south a low wall leaves windows and terrace open to the lively scenery. The terrace, an unusual feature, is divided into three, a rose-garden and two gardens of shrub roses, shrubs, tritomas and other flowering plants. It is paved and is the principal garden, other than a vegetable-garden.

10 Taptonville Road, Sheffield. Arthur Lee.
A town garden enclosed within high walls, a small sunken flower-garden leading to a fountain built into the angle formed by the junction of two converging walls.

Ward Green Community Park, Worsbrough Bridge, Barnsley.
A recreation park with sports facilities arranged so that they do not break into or spoil the long central glade. A formal terrace enclosed by dwarf walls, steps and bastions with seats.

SCOTLAND

Ardencraig, near Rothesay, Isle of Bute. Lord and Lady Colum Crichton-Stuart.
With extensive views over the River Clyde and the Kyles of Bute these gardens with the contrast of glades, formal walks and gardens, and with the heightened values of massed colour, are unusually varied in their charm and interest.

Drum-na-Vullin, Argyll. Miss Sylvia Campbell.
A short drive from the road brings one to the solid stone house. The river which flows through the garden is backed by steep banks of lilies, azaleas and other flowering shrubs. Crossing a stone bridge at the back of the house a path goes up and down the steep banks to connect across another bridge with the house lawn.

Falkland Palace, Fife. Major Michael Crichton-Stuart, M.C., National Trust of Scotland.
Hunting palace of the Stuarts. The new gardens have been designed to retain the palace and throw it into higher relief, and to preserve and bring into the scheme those traces of the earlier, more extensive palace buildings.

NORTHERN IRELAND

Aughentaine, Fivemiletown. Captain Hamilton-Stubber.
A new house was built on the site of the old castle. Near the house the drive skirts a small lake. There are a spacious forecourt, terraces extending for the length of the gardens on the higher level and, at the bottom of a steep bank, fine trees and walks between borders of flowering trees and shrubs.

WALES

Llanerch Park. Captain W. Piers Jones.
The house, standing in its own deer park, commands extensive views

over the gardens and the park and on to the river flowing in the valley below. From the highest terrace a flight of steps sixty feet long descends to a second terrace on which is a long, formal paved flower-garden. From here a second flight of steps descends to lower lawns and tennis-courts. There are, too, a long stream walk and extensive borders and gardens.

ETHIOPIA

The Imperial Palace, Addis Ababa. H.I.M. Haile Selassie.
The palace stands in its own grounds with extensive views from the windows into and over the gardens, the trees of which merge with those of the city park. There are formal water-gardens, a rose-garden, and lawn glades flanked by banks of trees and shrubs together making gardens varied in interest, lovely in themselves and a fitting setting for the palace.

AUSTRIA

Litzelberg, Seefeld. Mr. and Mrs. Clifford Curzon.
There are terraces, rose-garden and lawns onto which the house opens. There are also walks to and skirting the lake and back to the house, making a circular tour possible.

AMERICA

The British Pavilion, World's Fair, New York.
Erected on what had been the rubbish dump of New York. It was decided to have a typically English garden as a setting for the British Pavilion. It was designed somewhat on the lines of the gardens of the colleges at Oxford and Cambridge.

FRANCE

American Hospital of Paris, Neuilly.
With lawns, comparative spaciousness and a sequence of flowers against the green backgrounds of trees and shrubs, the grounds are an attractive setting for the buildings and a delightful pleasance for patients and staff.

La Bergerie, Les Hauts de St. Paul. Mons. Joseph Poupon.
At La Bergerie the terrace onto which the house opens extends to a loggia. There is a rose-garden. Flower borders lead to a swimming-pool, the social rendezvous of the garden, all partly enclosed by glades of flowering trees and shrubs.

Le Bungalow, Le Touquet. Arthur T. Kemp.
The garden for Le Bungalow at Le Touquet seemed to merge imperceptibly with the surrounding forest of pines and silver birches. Here was a rose-garden partly enclosed by a brick pergola, herbaceous borders and, on the western side, planted borders slightly Japanese in feeling. This garden was destroyed in World War II.

Cagnes, Lady Yule.

Because there is little if any winter in the English sense on the French Riviera, plant nurseries grow large trees in tubs. Planted with these trees Lady Yule's was a completely furnished garden from the time of planting.

The Cottage, Le Touquet. Arthur T. Kemp.

Practically every tree of Arthur Kemp's garden at Le Bungalow was destroyed in World War II and the house damaged. A cottage in the grounds was restored and gardens were made. With birches and pines, a long wide formal flower walk, a rose-garden and spreading lawns, the gardens merge with their setting of trees to make a delightful summer retreat.

GREECE

Athens. President and Mrs. Venizelos.

The new house built by the President and Mrs. Venizelos has two formal gardens, one at the back and the other bordering the Rue Kufuzzia. The gardens consist chiefly of lawns with borders of shrubs and flowering plants.

Index